D0762380

Thank you for choosing to read this portion of my memoir. I may or may not write more memoirs. This section of my life contains heavy, personal, trauma. I wrote this because my family was ripped apart by a monster. A monster that still feeds off the massacre with a bloody dripping grin. I have kept journals throughout my life and have time lined them into one book. This book was a toll on my mental health, so, when I finished writing it, I gave it one good review and edit, then I burned and deleted my old journals. I plan to never read this book again so I hope most of the mistakes were caught, but I know one edit, usually doesn't do the job. I hope that's understandable.

I am NOT omitting my past or pretending it never happened. I am proud of who I am and where I came from. I just don't need to carry the hurt in my head anymore so I wanted it out where I wouldn't forget it but also couldn't deny it. With this book I will never have to bring it up again, the truth is here for people to find without dragging me into the past.

The BEAST in the *Garden*

3

PART I

A Relevant Breakdown of the Background:

'White Noise'

Chapter 1 – Pre Pregnancy

A runt doesn't choose death, it's the cruelty of the environment that separates the resources for growth away from the runt rather than its siblings. Left to battle nature and nurture alone. But if the runt can survive, better yet adapt, to the lack of help, then they often thrive on even a simple amount or resources.

I was not born in a litter, but I was the runt of my siblings. Malnourished and pushed to the brink of death I lost everything. Raised by the image of an idol and a satanic dragon I was stuck in an illusion of hell, impaled by loyalty while burning in fire of jealousy and self-hate. But I am still alive and I hope that in releasing this story from myself I can get to that point of thriving.

My name is Tyrel but for the respect of most of the people in this memoir I will be using different names, and for the sake of matching the theme I will refer to myself, from now on, as Tyriel.

Everything has a cause and an effect, and to get to my effect I need to start with my cause. My father,

Hermes, was not talkative about his past, but this is what I know of the chemistry that brought me into the world:

Growing up in Minnesota on a farm, Hermes was a hardworking, rambunctious, and an unguided young German man who loved horses and valued loyalty and honesty. Looking for direction he joined the Air Force and was stationed to Madrid, Spain where he met Bastet, a beautiful Spanish dancer and got married. Later, I would discover she was also in the Air Force and from Florida, but she was, in fact, Spanish and she loved to dance (loved to party in general) and that's what Hermes considered the highlight of their meet-cute.

She became pregnant and he was ecstatic to have a child. Bastet cheated on Hermes with a coworker and the pregnancy resulted; she was not as excited to have a child. She admitted this and on the other end of a heated argument Hermes stayed. Hermes' Catholic upbringing looked down on divorce and he wanted to do anything to make it work. His love, and a promise of faithfulness from Bastet, kept his fatherly dream alive.

To better understand Hermes feelings I researched some marriage statistics and according to MarriageResourceCentre.org; in the 1970's, the percent of Americans married was 75%, and same-sex marriage would be illegal till 2015, so this was all hetero marriages. The divorce percent was about 50%. This number would be contested by the Catholic Church in the 2010's, stating the Catholic's percent was only 20% at that time. While the church brags about this percent it was a heavy reason my father was adamant to make the relationship work.

Bastet gave birth to the child and Hermes took her in as his own daughter. This newborn was not me, but my half-sister, Parvati.

Almost right away, Bastet became pregnant again, this time with Hermes' child and at about 7 AM on July 11th of 1983, I, Tyriel was born.

As my mother cradled me in her arms and smiled down on me, I can't imagine how tempestuous the thunderstorm in Bastet's mind turned. Maybe she yearned for freedom. A chance for a new life. Maybe she just loved paperwork.

She handed me to my father and said, "I want a divorce. I want you to have the child you always wanted, and I will keep Kichijoten."

I can only imagine the conversations and pleads made by both, but the divorce went through. Hermes felt as if I was an arranged birth to escape the relationship and viewed me as a victim of her greed and lies. He promised me, "I will never leave you. I will always be there for you. I will always love you."

Chapter 2 – Bumpy Beginnings

Bastet left the house with Kichijoten and Hermes hired a live-in-maid to help take care of me when he worked. Vac, an older Spanish woman, essentially my nanny, became my imprinted mother. She raised me for the first four years of my life. She kept me plump and cared for me, so much so, that I didn't know English; I spoke Spanish to English speaking father.

I have the vaguest memories of Vac and the only story I know of her happened at my age one. The bow in my right leg grew incorrectly, more details never came, and Hermes, who went to medical school, at the time, refused to take me in for it. My father became a physician's assistant, a PA, and I know many of his patients acclaim him to be the best medical professional to ever cure their body. As his son, however, he carried a pride about himself that kept him from asking for help. A superman complex that he also pressed on me, even as a one year old. "MY son couldn't possible have a growing disability."

I don't condone violence but Vac, a weaker older lady, took one of Hermes' heavy medical books and endlessly beat him, a young muscly cowboy, in the leg until he agreed to get me checked. He was not hurt at all but he did take me in to get a brace to fix a common leg twist; similar to Forest Gump's leg braces.

He didn't tell me this story until after I was grown and out of the house. For the first 20 years of my life I noticed my knees didn't face the same direction, just barely. When I brought it up to him, he told me he wanted me to 'assume I was perfect and could do anything without any excuses.'

When I was young he pushed me hard into sports and never let me say, "I can't do it," even if what I meant was, 'I don't want to do it.'

As far as I know, Vac was an amazing care taker and demanded wellness for me, but the military would set another move for Hermes, and Vac would not be coming with. Vac and I cried and clung to each other until we were physically separated. I never saw or heard from Vac ever again.

I wish her peace and happiness.

The government moved my father and me to San Antonio, Texas. Hermes became a more involved single parent. He carried his passion of the rodeo from Spain and became a cowboy, riding broncos and lassoing bulls. I appreciate a parent who can still have a social life with a child, but by himself, he was doing Air Force drills, medical school, parenting, rodeo, and partying with friends. He took me with him everywhere, for better or worse.

I don't know where he kept during his job and school, maybe they had nurseries, but he told me at the rodeo, girls flocked to him and begged to hold me and keep me company while he avoided horn stabbings and stampedes. Obviously in an attempt to get a date with an available Marlboro man, but my father liked being independent and playing the field. He was very attractive, worked out, sandy blond hair with a caterpillar mustache under a cowboy hat.

When he played ball with his mates I was there being thrown around like a football and he would require occasional plays that would get the ball to me

12

and allow me score a 'point'. I'm sure that was soo fun for his friends.

Even when Hermes went to the bar, the owner allowed him to bring me in, because Hermes lived above the bar and rented from him. I got to know the patrons. I don't know who took care of me when Hermes got drunk and he would get drunk often. Neither of us remembered much of this time.

Himself-admittedly, drank tons and spent a lot of time at the downstairs bar, including sneaking down after he thought I fell asleep. He told me a few stories of coming back from downstairs to find me up and out of bed eating a pie out of the fridge, or ripping up encyclopedia pages, or drawing on the wall plug-ins with permanent markers. The most certain memory I have of this time was a constant feeling Hermes would disappear, somehow, so maybe I was never fully asleep.

Once, he woke up on the bus stop bench in front of the bar; in the afternoon, missing wallet and keys. He sat up and carried himself to the apartment. I was found crying on the stairs and the apartment door was left open. He said this was the moment he decided

13

to clean up his act.

I've always known Hermes to drink quite a bit, on the daily, so I can only imagine how much more he drank at the time. I don't know his mindset, maybe he was always a party animal, but knowing him, I believe he hid the pain of losing his wife behind drinking, and kept other women away. When he found me on the stairs crying, he knew something needed to change.

Hermes carried the best intentions for me, while not understanding how to give them. For example, he desperately wanted me to be a famous football player so he made me sleep with a football instead of a teddy bear, so I would subconsciously know the smell and hold of the ball. He taught me a military-like-call back chant:

"Who do you love?"

"You."

"And who loves you?"

"You."

He promised me all the time that he was there for me, and he tried to keep that promise as best as I believe he thought he could.

One night, at the bar, Hermes and some of his colleagues were out drinking. I was upstairs, left alone again. One of his buddies was feeling lonely and Hermes suggested an attractive lady across the bar. The lady mistook Hermes' pointing and approached him instead of the friend. He turned her down not wanting to flip the script on his friend.

She returned the next night when Hermes was not with his friends and bought him a drink. They started up a conversation and she, Satan, entered our lives for the worse.

Chapter 3 – Susie is Satan

Hermes and I met Satan, a pretty Mexican college student in San Antonio, studying English. I debated sharing her race because I didn't want people to correlate her awful actions with her race, but this is a memoir and it becomes relevant further down the timeline, but to be clear, Satan is NOT a representation of her race, sex, or religion; she is just a shitty person.

I believe the bus stop-wakeup call opened Hermes to considering dating again and Satan struck with uncanny timing. She wedged her way into our lives and knew how melt his heart; by getting to mine.

The signs, invisible to me then, were subtle in hindsight. She buttered me up with gifts, and repeated how good a 'mom' she'd be while giving sly comments to Hermes, seeding how much he needed her;

"You can't dress him (me) like that. These things don't match. Let me dress him."

"You can't feed him fast food. Let me cook for you two."

16

"You can't have him live in this mess. Let me clean up."

"He needs a mother's touch." She managed to penetrate Hermes' thick independent pride. He wanted the best for me. How could he deny me help?

As Hermes tried drinking less, Satan replaced that time with her time, making herself available for babysitting while Hermes worked, schooled, and played. Using her indoctrinated strict St. Mary Catholic upbringing she convinced Hermes that she, as a woman, should be my natural care taker and he, as a man, should provide (money). My father, raised in a less harsh branch of Catholicism, yet still prepped by an 80's societal mindset, agreed.

Even though she was in school for a teaching degree, she was quick to prioritize Hermes' schooling. This cemented her presence around the apartment and Hermes viewed it as, "Satan sacrificed her own studies for me to get the grades that got me the job that feeds you." But I understand now how both, Satan and Hermes, fell under the binary Stone Age thinking of 'females gather and males hunt', keeping women second class 'family' prisoners for soo long in the world's history.

Hermes was an 'All-American' guy, privileged to fit the 'All-American' mold of that time. He followed the common path of school to military to a life-career with kids in a hetero-marriage, until retirement. Satan, with significantly less privilege, followed the much shorter 'All-American' gal path to find a husband, and have his kids.

As a side note, if someone wants to be a house-caretaker, by all means, I hope they get that life goal accomplished regardless of (or lack of) their gender. I'm more concerned with the woman-identifying people who DON'T want to do that but are forced into it via an eternal damnation that's manifested into their fears since childhood.

The best relationship advice I've discovered; Goals keep relationships active. If your only goal is to get a relationship, then you won't have a goal once you start the relationship. Figure out yourself and your goals first and find a partner with similar goals that you two (or more) can work towards. Trying to find ones goals with a partner(s) is limiting because, everyone goals, perspectives, and experiences in the relationship should be consider together. If done in the wrong order one can find themselves living for someone else, working for someone else, and dying for someone else.

Many times throughout this it will seem as if I am giving excuses to Satan's behavior. I am not, but I have tried very hard to see where she came from, and why this type of person exists. I don't believe in bad or good people, just a combination of bad and good actions, but Satan is the most consistent bad acting person in my personal life, to date.

To me. Satan is a monster because I became a target of her bad actions. I also think it's important to remind an outside perspective this is a portion of my memoir, my perspective. Satan might be the nicest person to everyone else on the planet, she certainly would love that character description; that does not discount my experience with her, but I'm getting ahead of myself.

Before she could sink her teeth in to me, I would be saved by a bigger, worse action, war.

Chapter 4 – A Kind Kin

I'm concerned of how this is legal, or maybe it's just another mystery of my past, but as an Air Force soldier my father needed to leave for a year and help in the war, Desert Storm, and I as a 4 year old, nearly 5, would need to FIND a place to live. I don't know what a soldier without a family would do, but thankfully Hermes called his sister in Minnesota and made accommodations. Hermes was sent across the world to Iraq, I was sent across the country to live with his sister in Blaine, Minnesota; basically a different planet.

My fear of Hermes leaving became real and his promise, although not his fault, was broken.

I lived with my aunt, Coatlicue for a year. She was a hair dresser and owned a salon inside her home. She tended a big veggie garden, and parented three daughters, my cousins; Clotho, Lachesis, and Atropos. They were 7, 6, and 4, respectively and I was newly 5.

Coatlicue was not prepared to temporally adopt a boy and the house didn't have any footballs, or trucks, or horses, or even toy guns! Instead their house was filled with all the things, as a little boy, I shouldn't be playing with; plastic dolls, fabric dolls, paper dolls, crayons and coloring books.

Memories are unreliable. At best a memory is a recalling of the last time you remembered that same thing and it's a game of telephone with your own thoughts. That is one reason why I like to write things down; a journal is the last most accurate telling of that memory. Besides some foggy, 99% error filled memories of my own, Hermes told me most of my past up to this point. At Coatlicue's house though I can personally recall my first most vivid memories:

Clotho, the oldest cousin, loved to dance and listen to music. We would jump on her bed, listen to songs on repeat and make up dance moves.

Lachesis was thoughtful, and taught me to make dandelion crowns. We played with the dolls, unjudged, and climbed all over an apple tree and a small swing set in the backyard.

Atropos, the youngest, had a huge coloring collection. We would create scenes and used the paper to create colorful, superhero outfits.

For Valentine's Day, I took red, pink and white construction papers and created a 'Heart Man' outfit and pranced around the house throwing paper hearts at people to help them fall in love.

While in Blaine, Coatlicue baptized me incase anything happened to Hermes. I remember bending backwards to have water placed on my head, because I was too big to pick up like a baby. It reminded me of my favorite part of Coatlicue giving me a haircut, the rinsing my loose hair at the sink.

I started kindergarten. I remember being excited for school, waiting in line with friends, and my teacher's short curly dark hair and thick glasses.

Then, one morning I was gently woken by my Aunt and she told me my father was sleeping on the couch in the living room, back from the war! I darted from my cousin's room and ran up the stairs and tackled Hermes and woke him from his slumber. He hugged and threw me in the air and we were rejoined. My first, soon to be second of five parental figures that have left (soo far), actually returned.

By age five I had a bio-mom, nanny mom, want-to-be-mom, god-mom and a father with priority issues; whether in his own control (drinking, hobbies, etc.) or out of his control (the Air Force, war).

Chapter 5 – Making a Marriage

I returned to Texas with Hermes and we met back up with a now graduated Satan. Although we were all happy to regather, Satan complained that Coatlicue baptized me.

Understanding the situation as adult, it makes sense for Coatlicue to become my god-mother in the very plausible case of Hermes' death. It makes no sense for Satan to be upset unless she already planned to become my parent and wanted me baptized under her. I point that out to prove after one year of dating (plus a year of an absence) Satan's goal was to marry Hermes. Not getting a job with her new degree, not dating more to confirm the compatibility, not learning how to live a life outside of school alone; she focused all of her manipulation skills on becoming a wife. Satan was upset about the baptism because she didn't and shouldn't have control at that time. Yet Satan claimed my aunt undermined her, and she used it to play victim.

"Coatlicue must not like me?"

"Women never like me."

Anything to fish for compliments and confirm Hermes' feelings audibly.

She didn't like that I enjoyed myself away from her. It had nothing to do with her but she took it personally and even after 20 years she will say what a mistake it was to have let me go to Coatlicue's house and get "twisted" by the lack of "control". She claimed the girl toys confused me and could turn me "queer". I believe this to be an excuse, along with the 'baptism disappointment', to push Hermes faster towards marriage.

The finishing touch; Satan became pregnant.

This didn't seem weird hearing their 'love story' when I was 10 or 15 but the more details came out, the soggier the puzzle pieces got.

My father was called back to war within three months of being back from war. I don't doubt they had sex, and it only takes one time to become pregnant, but she would have needed to get pregnant right away to start feeling it within LESS than 3 months. Yet, she felt the need to take a pregnancy test after a month! She claimed it to be a miracle that the day Hermes received the order to return to war she received a positive test.

Hermes was hesitant to marry because of his past marriage but he would be leaving for ANOTHER year, and now I had a brother on the way. Satan argued her religion looked down on pregnancy out of marriage; unfortunately her religion also looked down on contraceptives. Of course protection is not 100% effective, but this thought process and religious control added to how quickly she became pregnant, if this child was actually Hermes'.

Satan insisted they needed to get married NOW so she could keep me with her and my soon-to-be half-brother. If not, she would be left alone a single mother, without the ability to get a job (pregnant). She explained to me how she wanted to be my 'mommy' and how she was holding my brother in her belly. She idolized the brother role and made me feel special to become this title of older kin. When my father asked me what I wanted to do between her option and returning to my cousins, I felt obligated to make a family.

I was six and yet this decision would be held over my head for years and arguments to come, "You wanted her to be your mom. I asked you and you said yes."

It was then, during the beckoning of war, Hermes married Satan. They had a small Air Force wedding and he set her up to move into a new house on a different base he would meet her on when he returned.

She was taken care of now. No need for a degree, a job, no bills or skills, and she didn't have to deal with a husband; but she still had me to deal with and she made sure to treat me as her burden.

Before my seventh birthday, for the second time, my father left for a year. Back in Iraq, this time for Desert Shield. I once again moved across the country but this time to Bismarck, North Dakota, and this time with Satan. We moved into the second apartment of a fourplex; four skinny two story houses shoved into each other.

Satan gave birth and I had a little brother almost as a birthday gift. He was born two days before my birthday and Satan made him sound like the best present I could have. I felt proud to hold him in the hospital and I gave him the same shallow promise my father gave me, 'I'll never leave you', not fully understanding the promise or the irony of the missing person I mimicked.

Satan's family visited from Texas, excited to help for what they considered their family's first child. Satan and her sister's had an interesting bond. This new baby, my half-brother, Gaspar, was not the first child of their family. Technically, I was Satan's first, but even without counting me, Satan had a brother with three children. Those three children they considered belonged to their brother's wife, because they didn't have control of them. They didn't consider me her child, because I wasn't blood.

Satan and her sisters threw a celebration for Gaspar's birth. Two days later, when time to celebrate my birth, I was told by Satan's sisters that it was time for me to grow up and become a big brother to Gaspar. I was told how much Satan needed help and I would have to stop being 'needy' and I believed them.

They left shortly after, back to Texas, but I had learned how to change diapers, heat up and check milk, burp Gaspar, and of course I was his main entertainment as his older goofy brother. Satan was there watching every move to make sure I was doing it exactly how she wanted, and if I veered from those instructions she was quick to correct with a head slap or side poke. I don't know if it was the marriage, the new baby, or the loneliness, that triggered her abusive nature, but it never ended once it started.

Satan's need to control things annoyed her when she couldn't. While she got what she wanted (a husband and kid), it wasn't how she wanted it (rushed into a broken family with a husband at war.) These insecurities were taken out on me as I was both a reminder of her missing husband and a reminder of the imperfect family she started. The relevance of her skin color coming in now; Satan was dark skinned Mexican and Gaspar took on her dark skin. I had very white German/Spanish skin, and people, as people do, wondered where I came from in this family. This question drove her mad and steered her abusive motivations.

She didn't want to be seen in public and made me walk many steps behind or in front of her whenever at the store and she wanted me to call her 'Susie'. Her birth name was Jesusita Lira but her self-hatred came out as racism and she separated herself from her Hispanic background by calling herself the Americanized version: Susie. She told me her name (Jesusita) was the female Jesus and she didn't want others to know how special she was. Later when my father would arrive she would change her title to 'mom' insisting never to say 'step-mom.'

She didn't want the kids at school to ask questions so I learned to walk to and from school alone, at 7 years old. I didn't even know how to ride a bike yet, but she had me up waking myself up, dressed in the style she told me to, made my own lunch under her instruction (she didn't or couldn't pay the fee for school lunches.) I did my morning bathroom chores with proper measurements and egg-timers, and headed to school on time. The worse part of it, is she was STILL watching. If I stopped brushing my teeth before the timer went off, she would pop her head from around the door (doors were not allowed fully closed) and Satan would loudly scare me to correct my disobedience, sometimes yelling, sometimes just poking me in the side. She called it, 'breaking me down, to build me up.'

I mentioned I was excited to go to school a year before in Minnesota. Sure, it was kindergarten and now I was learning things, but the difference I noticed was the insertion of my anxiety and obsessive compulsiveness.

Satan berated Coatlicue's 'attempt' at making me representable for school. Although both Satan and Hermes came from low income families, Satan's lower than Hermes, she already forgot and looked down on those with less than her. She was graduated and married to a soon to be 'Doctor'; Coatlicue was 'white trash' with 'white trash kids' and Satan would never be viewed that way.

The day before the FIRST day of school, Satan ran me through chores but I messed a ham and cheese sandwich, I used the inertia to bring the mustard to the spout and it splattered out, onto the counter. She slapped my head and called me useless, but most impactful, she told me how stupid I was and if she was my age she would never talk to me or be my friend.

Satan began verbal and physical abusive; pulling my hair, pinching my arms and legs and poking my side with her sharp fingernails, leading me with my ears and nose, slaps, and spankings. She mocked me for crying for my father, because she knew I was crying to get away from her, while she also cried over the phone to her sisters if she made the right choice.

At 7, my Spanish was all but forgotten, Hermes didn't speak it, so it was never used except for Satan who was fluent and found it a helpful tool to keep secrets between her and her sisters. Satan went to school for teaching grammar and would also teach Spanish classes. When I asked her to teach me she would say, she didn't want to because she was talking to her sisters about where she hides treats and presents and she didn't want me to know. The treats would never be found and presents were not hid.

Eventually my father would return and when he did it was at night. He was quiet but Satan and I's celebration was not, and it woke Gaspar. She insisted

Hermes go greet Gaspar because his child 'should be able to recognize his father' despite the absence. He and Gaspar had never met. Her religion clouded her logic, and Gaspar screamed at the sight of a strange man coming into his bedroom with hands ready to pick him up. I think it was on purpose because it gave Satan the opportunity to swoop in and 'save' her baby. Hermes was heartbroken by the experience but I don't know what he expected.

Chapter 6 – Lesson in Lying

Along with the anxiety came a kind of paranoia. I'm not a medical professional and do not become one in the future (spoilers!) and while I have talked to a therapist about my anxiety I have never considered a diagnosis for any type of paranoia or an obsessive compulsive disorder. But whatever this paranoia was called, it formed because I was always under the eye of Satan, secretly being watched.

At home, at friend's house, at the store and school, Satan was secretly watching. At home she would hide around the corners to surprise-accuse me of being sneaky, even in the bathroom. If I was not in the house, she would call my friend's parents throughout my childhood, call my work under the guise of a customer, and she used her English degree to pop into my classes, letting the other teachers know she was a teacher and I should always be on my best behavior with a constant 'A'. If my grade ever fell below an A, she instructed the teacher to alert her and she will 'fix' the problem.

This warning would trigger an obsessive compulsive need to be perfect; I made sure from head to toe she would have the least to say about me and when that 'perfection' still couldn't be reached, that would trigger my anxiety. At 7, I didn't know what was happening; even now it's just an educated guess.

I equated a lack of negative attention with having to present 'perfect'. I hated being late because to me that caused a scene and then the whole class was witness to my bad behavior. I didn't like being called on for questions because what if I was wrong or didn't know the answer. I didn't go to the bathroom at all during school because I didn't want to disturb the class and pull focus on me. I already thought everyone was judging me so anything I could do to avoid performing and just be invisible became the new strategy.

I did not get all A's and it would be corrected. I would have to read my lessons allowed and write them. Literally, full chapters from the text onto paper, in addition to doing the homework sometimes up to three additional times. I would retake tests at home, make up tests, and write papers about my homework. Sometimes Satan would meticulously grade it and punish me further, because nothing was correct, or she would simply tear it up and be move on to something else, anything to keep me on my toes.

My father, was not completely absent. He was around for about three hours or less depending on homework or friends. He "let the wife, wife," and since he expected me to be a genius, he didn't see her as cruel, but harsh for progression sake. He must have thought something was amiss though, because he told her, "I don't mind you being this rough on Tyriel if you use the same discipline on Gaspar."

Later, when Hermes told me that, I was flabbergasted that he recognized her actions as 'rough' but instead of wanting her to be nicer he wanted her to maintain that roughness on the rest of the family?! Satan would also use Hermes' masculinity to keep me quiet by saying, "Stop crying. You don't want your dad to think you're a baby. Be a man." Seven years later Satan would NOT be treating Gaspar with the known level of abuse used on me, thankfully, but seven years later no one was keeping track.

At least Hermes vocalized his concern of Satan

letting me walk alone in the early morning to school and he got me set up on the bus system.

Another time, my eighth birthday and Gaspar's second, we received a shipment of presents from Texas. Satan's sisters went on a shopping spree for Gaspar and got me nothing. Hermes called them up and let them know, "If you are going to send gifts then you have to send gifts for both kids." He never, or was afraid of the answer, questioned if they had done the same thing the year before.

That following Christmas they sent the same shipload of presents but remembered to buy me a plastic cowboy gun with suction-cup bullets. Hermes called them up, again, to tell them the gifts had to be equal in value.

Three giant red flags his child was NOT being considered part of the family but he thought his instructions changed their programming. Another obvious red flag, to me, is that in his retelling of this phone call, he was the one that had to make the call and not Satan defending me; she agreed and probably knew prior to her sister's actions.

One day while waiting on the bus for its return to our houses, Satan's worse nightmare came true. A neighborhood boy integrated me on why I was so white in comparison to 'my mom'. Satan started demanding I call her 'Mother' to keep up the illusion (never with a 'step' in front). I did, but I didn't understand why and without calling her step I described how she was a step. I didn't even really care if people knew, except the boy was mean and started calling me names like 'egg baby', and 'fake mommy'; stupid names that hit a nerve with my mama drama.

I was the kid that kept smiling and laughing through the pain and agreeing with the insults, until my perfect wall couldn't sustain itself anymore and a panic attack would take over. I lost control of my emotions and bawled. The bus driver had me sit up front and reorganized their stops to drop me off first and I went home trying to hide my tears. I kept a straight face but the caring bus driver called later to make sure I was okay and I saw the devastation hit Satan's face as she realized her secret was out!

She hung up the phone and attacked me grabbing me by the scruff of my neck with her short sharp claws digging into the back of my neck, she yelled down at me how stupid and worthless I was. How troublesome I was to tell people our family dynamics and I was an embarrassment for crying. I was crying again and she stopped herself from removing the skin her nails were ready to scoop out. Instead she fed me a jalapeno for not being able to keep secrets and sent me to my room without dinner. When Hermes got down with work, she told Hermes I told everyone at school she was my step-mom and now our family was viewed as broken and her "reputation" was in danger.

To be clear; I'm inclusive and love the fact that we have different representations of families in the world. I didn't see a problem with mine and both Hermes and Satan explained the situation fine to me for me to accept it. I don't know why this was a point of contention for Satan, but when she got that call, and the bus driver told her what the insults were about, her reaction was to run; she wanted to move.

Satan told Hermes that she was afraid for MY safety. I would continue to be bullied and have no friends. Hermes, being in the army had an option to move coming up and agreed a new start would be helpful. They both talked to me about keeping our 'broken' step-family a secret and we practiced scenarios to perfect the story. I would say, "Gaspar got my mom's dominant genes and I got my dad's dominant genes." I didn't know what that meant so it didn't solve the problem but that was the plan. We would even lie to Gaspar. My parent's would start telling people they got married eight years ago, six years earlier than they had and one year before I was born to 'make it make sense.'

Prepared or not, we would be moving to Texas and the anxiety, abuse, and fatigue would get worse as Satan got more bold with her sisters near.

Chapter 7 – The First Fissure

Wichita Falls, Texas was my least favorite place to live. Not because of the people or the places, but I went from a few friends to absolute zero friends. This is the year I was the most introverted. My plan to become invisible worked and I hated it, but it felt better than the anxiety of being noticed.

We moved off base and Hermes would drive further to work while Satan's sisters would visit daily to play with their 'Golden Boy'. The favoritism was running high but they kept it from Hermes' senses. Satan's actions were rubbing off on my brother. As soon as he was walking he was also punching and hitting on me. I was required, by Satan to take it because I should, "Be a man," and "learn to take a punch." He would run up to me, mimicking Satan, and yell incoherently (he is a two years old) grabbing a fist full of my hair in one hand and hitting me with a toy in the head with the other, while Satan laughed about how much a 'wussy' I was and how 'strong' her little boy was.

I was watching TV when a Gaspar was attacking and I pushed him off me and he got hurt falling down. It was my fault he fell but nothing serious came of it, until Satan darted into the room, she was watching from the kitchen, and slapped me four or five times, back and forth and yelled, "Never lay your hands on my boy!" She gave Gaspar ice-cream and sent me to my room. I'm aware now, the ice-cream was not for Gaspar, it was for me to know I was not getting any.

There was a point I thought Satan was an idiot. I would cry to Hermes about her abuse and tell him I didn't want to be with her anymore, but he would tell me I made that choice and 'we don't quit.' He would love to say phrases with our last name in them; Bergmann's don't quit, Bergmann's don't lie, Bergmann's value loyalty. Satan followed none of these, but I realized she never showed her abuse towards me, in front of Hermes. She knew she what was doing and when to do it; I was the 9 year old idiot. I thought I could catch her without proof. When she was awful I was excited that 'ha' she had said one thing to my father and now she was hitting me again, but of course a 'good' witness was never around. She simply denied it when I brought it up, and I would get in more trouble later. I didn't know what gas lighting was then, but that is when I noticed it and started journaling. To check my own sanity.

I also was unaware of the Cinderella effect. Wikipedia defines this effect as, 'the phenomenon of higher incidences of different forms of child abuse and mistreatment by stepparents than by biological parents.' Obviously a wink to the fairytale with the evil step mom that loves her gene pool kids and the riches she married into but despises and abuses the stepchild that came with those riches.

The abuse became sexual as well. I won't go into great deal, but being born in Spain, I was not circumcised and needed to pull back my foreskin for upkeep. I was nine and doing soo many things around the house for myself and my brother but Satan didn't trust me to clean my own penis apparently. If any of my parents should have been cleaning my penis for medical reasons, maybe the one with a penis who is also medically trained, but no. She would have me stood up in dirty bath water (shared with Gaspar) and pull my skin back to the max sometimes tearing it. I wasn't allowed to move as she scrapped at it with her nails and if I did move or say 'ouch' she pinch the tip of my exposed penis while telling me both, "this is for your own good," and "I'll show you what pain is." She would make many contradictory ambiguous statements like that when defending her punishments for me. I would wake up the next morning with a crotch that crusted from the plasm being squeezed out of my stretch skin and cuts, which she would then take pleasure in pouring alcohol over and additionally tell me, "See, this is why I have to do this to you." Conveniently then, she would also tell me to not let anyone touch me there and to let her know if anyone ever did. She was hiding her most obvious abuse in a place where she could appropriately convince me not to talk to others about it. She did this for at least two years until I was able to convince my dad I can shower by myself. Satan would still have the bathroom door open and make surprise visits to make sure I wasn't getting comfortable. I would still have an order in which things had to be done and timers to be used for the shower, brushing my teeth, washing my hands and face, and styling my hair. She would still expose me nude to my brothers or her sisters and mock my body.

44

One night, before I showered alone, I was crying in bed and Satan had her sister's over. One of the sister's walked by the room and heard me crying and asked Satan about it. Satan came into my room, flicked on the light with a mean smile and made eye contact with my wet eyes. Her face turned demonic, grey and wrinkly with sunken eyes, I was terrified but then she slapped me and the image was gone. She held a finger to her lips for me to be quiet and turned the light off and left, closing the door behind her. I heard her tell her sisters I was just singing myself to sleep and to ignore me. I still envision her 'real' face and wonder what I saw that night. I never saw it again though, no matter how hard I looked for it.

Satan, true to her motto, was still trying to 'break me down to build me up,' and after only two years of her as my mother, it was working.

One day, we got a phone call that tossed Satan in a tizzy; my bio-mom, Bastet, was driving through Texas for a work gig and wanted to visit. Apparently Bastet and my half-sister, Parvati, had been writing me letters and while I responded to them in the past it was about 5 years and she wanted to make sure I was okay.

45

Hermes had kept in touch with her, but Satan wanted Bastet gone. And she told her so. Satan told her, that her presents was harmful to me, confusing for me, and ruining the life she, Satan, was trying to create (aka exposing the illusion).

I was not there for the conversation; Hermes would tell me about it when I would ask of Bastet, but I would not see her for the rest of my childhood.

Soft **trigger warning**, but still a warning:

This was the most depressed time of my life. I've had deeper, darker times, but at 9, with little understanding of the world and a lack of power in my own life, I carried an unrelenting sadness. My dad gave me a complement that later I would consider an insult, I'm the 'most adaptable person' he knew.

I was not adaptable; Satan broke me down. Maybe it was a switch from an open-minded, loving environment with my Aunt Coatlicue, to the restricted, paranoia-inducing nightmare attached to the Warden Satan. I was a happy kid, who couldn't find happiness. In a new place, with no one to talk to, I didn't want to be in the world any longer. I believed in a vague idea of a heaven that sounded better than here. Keeping in mind I was 9, I took a wool red blanket and laid in the street, under it, waiting for a car to run me over. I found a shady spot, the road sizzled but within seconds a nosey neighbor ran outside to figure out what I was doing.

I didn't admit to it at the time, out of embarrassment, but the neighbor suspected enough to tell my parents and my father teared up reminding me of his promise that we would 'never leave each other'. He told me what a sin suicide was, and how it was a sure way not to get into heaven, and it's an action we must never do. "No situation is that bad."

The silver lining of my suicide attempt is that it ruined Satan's reputation (in her head) and she would want to move again. She wanted to move even closer to her sisters at the Air Force Base, in San Antonio. When the opportunity to move annually came up, Hermes applied, but in the Air Force, where you want to move is only a suggestion and instead of Satan's choice we moved to the east coast; Langley, Virginia.

Chapter 8 – Rising Rebellion

Before we set our feet in Virginia, I mentally prepared to battle my anxiety, known to me as 'nerves', determined to not be the sad lonely boy in the corner of the class. We were moving on an Air Force Base again and surely there would be other kids. I would force myself to learn how to be social.

Hermes was certainly capable of identifying signs of anxiety and he must have known what it was by this time in his medical journey, but he refused to believe his kids would have anything wrong with them. It was the denial of my Forest Gump leg all over again, except this time Vac (my Spanish nanny) was replaced with Satan, and Satan was not there to defend my wellbeing. It became a running joke in our house that if we ever got seriously hurt we already knew what Hermes would say, "Can you move it?" and our answer was always yes, "Then it's not broken." Horrendous advice by the way, I've seen a dog try to eat with a broken face, and broken things CAN and do move. If we were ever choking we were conscious enough not to say, "I can't breathe!" because his response would be,

"If you can talk, you can breathe." Nevertheless, physical or mental disabilities were 'above' us, so anything I had went undiagnosed. In another surprise turn, Hermes proudly told me he had signed off on my immunization shots for school and I had NEVER had them. I've had that corrected since then, but why? 'Why' to all of that.

I remember, my parents were unpacking, I was soo proud of myself to walk through the sliding glass door and begin my search for friends. Anxiety was right by myside but I felt confident. We lived in one of four apartment buildings that squared off a block, surrounding a field with a playground. Ten steps out of my house onto the perimeter of sidewalk, a punk kid walked by and looked me up and down before saying, "Nice shoes homo," and kept walking. My first homophobic encounter. I had no idea what it meant, Satan dressed me, and I while I could rant on about her JC Penny's catalogue fashion of the 90's; her bad taste in clothes is the least of my complaints. I kept walking in my direction, less strong.

At the playground, a lanky blonde girl sat on the top of a metal hexagon ball. She also looked me up

49

and down, and curiously said, "Hi." We got to know each other, and she knew all the other kids in the other complexes and I had a group of friends again, including the punk kid. My house was still hell but I had an escape, and with new perspectives, room to grow; socially and pubescently.

Satan responded to my social activity by tripling down on her attack. She either didn't take my 'lame' suicide attempt seriously or didn't care, or a third option - cared to kill. Once again as the new kid in school, wanting to make friends, Satan was my demotivational blow horn in my ear every morning. She'd call the spaces in my teeth, 'Chainsaw Mouth' and offered me Chiclets to fill the gap. As mentioned before, my braced leg never fully healed and the strut it put in my walk would have her singing, "'V' is for Victory" almost every time I walked into a room without consciously correcting myself, into my 30's. It became a theme song and this would be sang in front of people with her knowing that it could sound like a compliment, but I would know she was referring to by busted leg stance.

"Dumbo" was a popular name for when she

pulled or flicked my ears, and 'Pinocchio' for my big nose or when she wanted to accuse me of lying. Insults to ruin things I liked. Most ironically, she would call me Cintyrella.

I wouldn't come out for almost a decade later and Satan (despite the insults) insisted she couldn't tell I was gay, but she was always slapping my hands to put them on my sides rather than limp wristed in front of me. She hated my voice for being nasally and effeminate and mimicked my lisp. She teased me for the way I laughed and YAWNED! And the saddest part is I either believed her, or simply wanted her approval so she would stop abusing me, either way, I actually changed.

I practiced different laughs, I learned to yawn inside my mouth, I kept my hands to my sides and I even trained myself to walk with my feet parallel and articulated my words harder. She quite literally, with my attempt at leaving this life, broke me down and she was now 'building me up' how she wanted me to be.

Or so she thought.

I was surviving her, and learning to 'adapt' to the situation. I said I grew to consider 'being adaptable' an insult. I saw it as, 'being able to easily change for other people's comfort' or 'getting used to abuse' instead of standing up for yourself, because that's what I found myself doing.

She called me a robot a few times but I smoothed it out, but she must have sensed something still a little gay, because she bought me a pendant of a Jesus and wanted me to start going to church with her to reinforce the 'manliness' I lost from hanging out with the blond girl at the playground. Looking back now, I realize her claim of not being able to identify me as gay is because she believed gay to be a choice, she didn't think any child could consider being gay until they choose to be.

Oddly enough this is the first time I got a crush, and it was of course on a boy, because I'm a gay. He was a punk kid, friends with the other punk kid that called me homo. He introduced me to the Terminator and Alien(s), D&D, Video Games, and Modern Music. At home, I was only allowed to listen to country music of an older generation, singing and dancing was ridiculed, and no movies but Disney. The Little Mermaid was my favorite movie, a child held tight under her parent's rule that longed to be part of a different world. My television reached two channels PBS and channel 3, to play video games on.

Video games...my true first crush. Satan didn't play anything but Mario a couple times, and thought video games were innocent enough. Most of my entertainment was centered on what a 3 year old could do since Gaspar was Satan's priority. If I could get into it, I could bring it into the house. But video game art, for the most part, looked cartoony enough even if it was not age appropriate, not to say that it wasn't age appropriate for a less strict guardian.

I would go to the boy's house (I liked) and my mind would explode with all the cool sci-fi. He was an aggressive kid with tons of energy and loved to get rambunctious. He was always punching and jumping on me, which I didn't care for but he pinned up against a wall once under the complex stairs and held me there for a moment. Nothing else happened, physically, we went on to play whatever game, but sexually something awoke in me. I would react the way Hermes had taught me...deny its existence. My logic worked like this; Homosexuals are evil and going to hell. I'm not evil and I'm not going to hell. Therefore, no homo.

I didn't know what a gay was other than Satan yelling a slur at a portrayal of a one on television, and even then I didn't know what made them gay, other than those mannerisms I had displaced. I also didn't know what love was or felt like, so when I felt this attraction to another male, I didn't know it was a crush or gay. I just knew my heart beat different, around him in particular, and I liked it. If I thought it was gay I might have tried to avoid it, but I had a perspective problem.

I, still now even, assume people have similar experiences to me. I believe this worldview comes from being afraid to ask questions due to my isolation from others because of Satan and myself, and the dismissive attitude of Hermes. I assumed anxiety was a normal feeling we all dealt with and I just needed to figure it out like everyone else had 'apparently' done. I assumed all guys had attraction to guys and just didn't speak on it. I assumed parental abuse was normal. I assumed everyone had home problems we didn't discuss because it was common place. I assumed no one was a victim of circumstance.

Maybe I made these assumptions because when I would complain to my father he would tell me a similar story of his past to relate and then his advice was "that's life." Once when complaining about Satan, he gave me a story about his time in 'training' (in the Air Force) and a drill sergeant that would yell and punish him no matter how well he did. And Hermes' advice; "I dug down and did better and proved him wrong."

I assume the whole army base camp threw off their hats and cheered for him.

Chapter 9 – Jamming with Jesus

Here, in Virginia, Satan and Hermes would have their second child together, Melchior. Gaspar was not yet in school so Satan insisted on not working and now with Melchior she would be resetting her timer and pushing back her career.

Satan used her religious background and society's expectations and leaned into them hard to insinuate control over the family. Satan decorated the house with her aesthetics and any of Hermes' family items or suggested tastes was insulted and thrown out.

I didn't understand at the time the mental abuse she was putting Hermes through. I don't think he did either and if he did he was too 'manly' to admit it. A report done via Criminology studies called 'Effect of Religion on Domestic Violence Perpetration among American Adults (by Cassidy Mitchell in 2019) says, 'Women who attend services at least once a week were about 44.2% less likely to report domestic violence against a partner.' This percent would definitely be higher in the 1990's and they do not stat 'men', which I know would also be higher based on toxic masculinity.

Food and clothes were bought and arranged by her for everyone in the family. Our time, including play time, was scheduled. Satan controlled 100% of the household and it would only be fair to give her the 100% credit for the environment and atmosphere. I thought, then, that Hermes and Satan were on the same page, but she lied about her intentions when he called her out on her impact. I do blame Hermes for believing her, I blame Hermes for turning a blind eye, and I blame Hermes for thinking a good job makes a good dad; but he wasn't abusive or purposefully mean. He was also abused mentally and emotionally by her. She used the children and her maternal 'role' to take power of the finances and control the stress levels of the house with the threat of looming outbursts.

She was likely to rage, now I understand she was getting mad drunk, at least once a week, and it was a display for the family. She didn't time out in her room or vent to her sisters. She was in the living space either hitting or slapping (some form of physically assault) at either me or Hermes. She's broken an assortment of household items, from cassettes to

57

windows, and this is when her most vicious insults would spit until she passed and woke apologizing to him, rarely me.

Regardless, looking back I will give her the credit for raising me and her other kids as ableists, sexists, homophobes, transphobes, speciesists, racists and privileged, spoiled, ignorants…at minimum. And I can personally credit her for my anxiety, trust issues, sleep paralysis and nightmares (involving her). In addition to my survival tactics to block a door in the bathroom with an extended drawer or trash can, the ability to hide emotions of pain, surprise, or even joy, not to mention (but to mention) being triggered by jalapenos, my naivety on the world, self-hate and of course a 'cute' laugh. All this by ten; Mother of the Year.

We only lived in Virginia for a year and I left all those friends behind to do the social dance again; again in Texas, this time San Angelo, not to be confused with San Antonio much to Satan's dismay. We would be here for the next five years. Satan would have her third and last child with Hermes, Balthasar, and Hermes would retire from the Air Force after 20 years. But I'm getting ahead of myself, before of all that we moved into a haunted house! (I don't know what to believe here, it's some interesting stories but not relevant to this part of the memoir, but maybe I'd include it in a 'search for the truth' memoir because it's a big part of my quest for answers. For now I'll just say-) The house was not on the Air Force Base, very cheap, and weird things happened there that I, as an 11-16 year old, could not explain; and that's all I knew WHILE living there; I found out more about the history of the house only after we would move out later.

Every place we moved, since North Dakota (Wichita, Langley, here, and future places), people asked about the family's dynamics. Balthasar was darker than Gaspar and Melchior was darker than both of them. I thought it was cool that we had such an arrangement of color, however, I was still pointed out as the 'white one'. Especially when Satan's sisters were around shouting, "Gringella!" a combo of gringo (white guy) and Cinderella, obviously coined by Satan.

It would have helped if my father was around more, for the reasons of being a better parent, yes, but also so people might've had a better visual of where

59

this white looking child came from. But Satan's reaction to their simple questions is the issue, not how the situation could have been avoided.

I would blatantly lie to strangers (and my brothers) as we grew up, under Satan's instructions. The strangers knew I was lying, most of them. No one truly cared about or the answer or Satan's fed lies. They just wanted to start a conversation, maybe in an over personal way, but not in an intentionally, offensive way.

Satan was not there to make friends though, I don't think she wanted friends. Her and her sisters were enough for each other. In all the places we lived, Satan didn't become friends with a single neighbor or extended friend of Hermes. She talked about Hermes' friends behind their back, told Hermes he shouldn't hang out with them, and argued making them avoid the house, particularly any neighbor we shared a line with. No one came over, no one saw her decorations or shared in a dinner; not once.

I, on the other hand, desperately wanted out of the house and did find friends. Using what I learned from the last place, I started up awkward conversations with the neighborhood kids and built friendships I still have today. As I started middle school, 7th grade, this new middle school carried the grades 7 through 9 (it's not the same across the country). Gaspar was just starting kindergarten and Satan wanted to hold me back a year so that Gaspar would feel comfortable in the elementary school. Thankfully Hermes pointed out that we would be in different wings of the school and never see each other anyway. She didn't push further.

In middle school I met good friends that were nerdy, cinematic, and overall kind. I also joined the choir and began my love for music. I got to listen to the forbidden 'pop songs' and sing amongst other singers. I took Art classes and rediscovered my passion for drawing and color. I even joined theater despite my over whelming fear to get on stage and learned more about fashion. Past interests that I had been drawn to when living with Coatlicue. Happiness offered again, I found enjoyment for life, but only outside of the house.

A bigger **Trigger Warning**.

A friend taught me how to tape one side of a

music cassette to record the radio over the audio; changed my life. I would sneak into Hermes' office and use his boom-box to record songs and use his walk-man to listen to those songs under the covers before bed, being very careful not to hum. Satan found them and they were just gone. No acknowledgement of them, just the walk-man back where it was from, and a nest of cassette tape in the trash and a newly locked office door. If I liked it, she would take it. I knew I would need to pretend to like nothing or just enjoy things for the moment, knowing they wouldn't last. There was a third option that I reconsidered as I stared at the road waiting to go to school one morning. I thought about my past suicide attempt. Although I was excited to go to school, I knew classes would end and that outlet would be gone. I would be left with Satan twisting my arm skin to 'look happier', or step on my toes because they are 'too big" and I'm ugly. The bus came.

I made up my mind at school and by the afternoon, I was going to take my own life. I'd be smarter about it, and not leave it up to another passerby or a witness looking out the window. Satan left with my youngest brother, Balthasar, for groceries and I was babysitting the older two, Gaspar and Melchior.

I put them in a room with flavored icees and put on Aladdin. I then went to the kitchen and pulled a big knife from the drawer, and before I could think to stop myself I thrusted it at my chest.

Chapter 10 – Winning with Weakness

Maybe it was a 'miracle' or most likely the lucky aim of a very weak 13 year old; the knife caught in the grooves of the Jesus pendant and prevented me harm. I opened my eyes confused and, with tears running down my cheeks, checked my chest and the necklace. The knife didn't even pierce the pendant. I was left without soo much as a paper cut. I put the knife back with a new perspective.

I was indoctrinated at this point and believed it was a sign from above that this Jesus shield saved me. I told myself then I would never attempt to kill myself again. There must be something I didn't know about that this Jesus or a god wants ME to be around for. While I don't think that way now, I am appreciative for the self-love I needed at that time to survive. It's not beyond my irony though, the same belief I chose to now live for is also why I was soo quick to leave and go to a 'happier place' in the first place.

Since then, for the sake of other's worry, I have not gone back to that thought process or feelings, even while putting down the belief of a god. I love living and life and learning; I wasn't at this healthy spot yet.

I would need this new lease on life because Satan's wrath grew as she picked up drinking. Fireball was a hidden bottle of choice.

Everything I did bothered Satan; I mentioned her correcting my mannerisms, but now she was complaining about my breathing! She convinced my father I was breathing too loudly and needed surgery. I wasn't having trouble breathing, it was just too loud for her. I ended up receiving septoplasty, a surgery to fix a deviated septum. It didn't change anything but it did give her an excuse to make fun of my now crooked nose and call me "Picassnose". This didn't prevent her from still grabbing my broken nose and leading me around with it or telling me I must be a liar because my nose is soo big. She constantly called me a liar to make me question my own reality and she told me why I must be one- there were signs; my nose is big, my nails have white moon shaped marks, I'm looking to the left or right, or even she prayed on it and god told her the truth. All of these were ways of making me and others doubt myself when I complained about her actions.

Somehow, through the gas lighting, I never thought I was a 'bad' person. I really wanted to be, and tried very hard to be, whatever definition of 'good' Satan held; be like a Jesus. I was never violent, not even sporty competitive (my anxiety would not allow me to enjoy sports). I never cussed and was trained to be respectful; Satan perfected my manners and taught me to blindly listen to authority, Hermes reinforced the view with his military training. I wasn't messy, I was essentially the maid. However, to Satan, I was an embarrassing, disrespectful, annoyance that she had to babysit and excuse.

I'm not claiming innocents. I've lied, many times; maybe even enough times to call me a 'liar', but I have done research on lying and where lying comes from. Kids can be trained to lie. Kids naturally lie from 2 to 8 (PBS.org). It's a way to "test the reality of the world, exercise imagination and test communication." There are healthy ways to promote and model truth-telling just like there are ways to promote lying, but I won't go over all of them because it's still in scientific discovery. However, we DO know, intense punishments that do not correlate with the action the child has done creates a high-risk/high-reward gamble most children are willing to take. Unfortunately, for the child, when you are dealing with a narcissistic parent, the house will always win.

Some of the punishments Satan came up with: Withdrawal from choir, wooden spoon spankings, bad haircuts, picking dandelions during a rain or lightning storm, pouring jalapeno juice on open sores, cold showers, dressed in girl clothes (she bought) and mocked, displayed nude to brothers and guests, food taken away, public humiliation, etc. Those are some of the punishments I can guarantee. I'm sure there are many unnoticed complexities in my life that Satan orchestrated or I'm still unpacking as abuse.

Like I said before, she claimed she never saw the signs of my gayness (almost 5 years from coming out) but she used all the insults a little gay boy would here from a parental bigot. "You do [action] like a girl/pussy/baby/wimp," "be a man," "you're overly sensitive" etc. In addition to bullying me, her paranoia and loneliness caused her to belittle my friends; other 13 year olds. Satan gave them nicknames mixing their names with an insult on their looks or something about

67

how trashy they were; her favorite insult.

Hermes was not visible happy anymore either but would not admit it. He enabled Satan's actions by saying she had a hard childhood and she means the best, or I'm misinterpreting her 'love', combined with, "she's stressed out right now" and "she'll be in a better mood later". They had begun to argue more often and more intense. She wanted attention, so she would try to control more aspects of his life and he escaped her by working more. On top of finishing up medical school, heavy studying almost nightly, Air Force duties, a medical job, and bowling, Hermes picked up a second medical job on the weekends at a hospital an hour away. He would spend nights at and I was witness a few times to say It was a real job; he wasn't cheating as he was suspected multiple times, at least when I was there, he wasn't cheating. It was boring most of the time but sometimes an emergency would come in that would make things hectic; but it was an escape. I wondered if that's how Hermes viewed it also.

Satan was great at snide, petty remarks, and under the belt digs. Hermes, in a sexist mindset, thought 'let crazy, be crazy', "this is what marriage is like," "sometimes to tame your woman, you just got let her shout." –The beginning of my bad dating advice.

On a, I'm sure, romantic, evening date between the two, they left me behind as babysitter. The youngest brother, Balthasar, fell asleep. I took him to his crib and enjoyed video games with my other two brothers until our parents got home. Satan came in the house, twisted from alcohol and asked where Balthasar was. When I replied he was asleep in bed, she flew off the handle. She yelled at me to wake him, "He is going to wake up in the middle of the night and keep ME up. You put him to bed too early!" She was slapping me and shoving me out of the room towards the bedroom and I went to pick Balthasar up. I heard Satan still screaming about it in the other room to Hermes as he got entered the house. I walked into the kitchen and Satan grabbed the knife, I previously tried to kill myself with, and lunged at me! I was holding Balthasar; I don't know what she intended to do, but I turned to protect my smallest half-brother while my father tackled her from behind and wrestled the knife from her hands.

He managed to take the weapon from her only

after getting his hand sliced open. She went to the bedroom and passed out, and he left me ALONE with her, to drive around and think about the situation. This was typically how they handled an argument. Satan would spew abuse, usually in the form of verbal insults and physically attacks only to eventually pass out, and Hermes would dash away in his car to cool down.

All four brothers would be told that these were part of the secrets we should keep in the family and not talk with friends or other adults about. "Every family has their problems. We do not air our dirty laundry." These were not once or twice scenarios, they happened throughout my life, but I want to take this moment to give a friendly reminder that this memoir is not a pity party; it's not even particularly rare, unfortunately. Ideally this memoir will do two things:

Clear the lies and untangle the story Satan webbed around our family and;

Alert more people to the Cinderella-Effect, Narcissism, Abuse and the power to see something and say something (especially nowadays, with the ability to learn nearly anything via the internet.)

I'm not naive enough to think the internet will eliminate the hateful bigotry people like Satan hold, but I do hope it helps call those people out and hold them responsible for the devastating actions they keep in our own community's growth and members.

I was a fool for the first fifteen years of life, understanding I didn't like the abuse but normalizing it. If someone would have called it out, Satan would not have stopped, but I would have witnessed someone agreeing with me instead of feeling like I was wrong for thinking the abuse was wrong. The phrase, "You don't deserve that; you have a bad parent," would have brought a different understanding to my upbringing.

This is also a suggestive plead to potential parents to research how to raise a child before having it. Our society is famous for saying, "you'll just figure it out," or "There's not a book on raising children," but that is wrong. There are many books and we have research; how spankings effect children, how denying self-identification attributes to depression and suicide, how to spot abuse. We have created agencies that can help walk someone out of an abusive situation.

If having a baby is priority or if the act of raising a child is considered 'the most important job', then it would be absurd not to put in the effort of doing research to ensure that important job is done correctly.

Chapter 11 – Invisible Insight

In 99', Hermes retired from the Air Force and was offered a final free move. My father's plan was to move to Texas as often as the Air Force allowed it, BUT when he retired he wanted to return to Minnesota, his home state, buy land and start a farm. He was excited to raise his four boys on said farm, like he had been, and teach us to ride horses, like he had done. (Still pushing his life goals on his children despite our four different personalities and wants.)

The thought of leaving Texas (her sisters) and not having the option of another move for a while scared Satan. During an argument in the car between her and Hermes on the topic, she ended the conversation by crashing the car into another parked car in a grocery parking lot. Only Hermes and Satan were in the vehicle and Hermes didn't go into detail about the argument other than Satan could have been blinded by the air bags (breaking her sunglasses); he was more concerned about Satan's safety, as a good husband would be. That was her plan, remind him what was 'really important', but the argument didn't go away. They brought it home and she threw plates, the phone, the vacuum cleaner, shoes and food. She was determined to destroy the house if she couldn't live here anymore.

I was with my brothers in our 'playroom' area, watching a sing along, when Satan tornadoed in and kicked over the baby railing separating us from the rest of the house. She grimaced at me before yelling how "none of this (the items in the house) would be here without her," and none of it was "deserved." She ripped the VCR (the machine playing the movie) from the stand and pulled the cords from it. She threw it at Hermes as he came into the room after and he surprisingly caught it (I remember thinking how cool that was and imagining me doing something similar during a fight with her). I grabbed Balthasar up from the floor and ushered my other half-brothers outside (the only available exit) since the movie was clearly over. Satan grabbed me from behind and pulled Balthasar from my hands, scratching him on the face, above the eye. He was already crying but his louder hurt cry stopped her rage. She yelled at me for hurting him, but thankfully Hermes saw the truth, and she didn't carry on. I've wondered what could have happened had he not followed her; if he took a drive like he normally did. Luckily, the car had been busted.

Nevertheless, the decision to move came down to me. I don't know why my father insisted on making me the decision breaker for life changing choices. It encouraged Satan's thoughts that I was responsible for her unhappiness. I get wanting to have my input. My input, and everyone's involved should be heard, but as the parent, who has (and is not willing to share) all the information, our input should only be part of the whole picture that helps the guardian decide. Their immaturity to come to a choice, brought the weight and blame on me and gave Satan more reason to hate me.

I, primed to move, liked moving. Despite my anxiety, I liked meeting new people, and I liked beating my anxiety, I wanted a horse, and I still hoped to find a happy home.

I chose to move, and we moved to Long Prairie, Minnesota.

Satan 'agreed' to moving, but brought demands

to the situation: She would not live in a house someone else lived in (this was a combo of the haunted rumors of this current house and entitlement), she wanted to design the next house, and any farm on the location should be away from the house-preferable out of sight (behind a hill or forest). Those were the main ones and none of them stopped Hermes' excitement.

She refused to leave Texas until the house was built and designed, so Hermes and I went to Minnesota ourselves to start the process, and we lived in a trailer park for about three months while a Satan-designed basement and garage were dug. The first floor of a house was bought and brought to the new land to put on the basement and we built up a second floor and an attic.

I got my first job, under the table, as a 'handyman' around the trailer park. I was 15 then, but as my birthday was coming up in July, I had my first 'over the table' job the day of. Once again, I'm new in town with no friends and new at work. No one knew it was my birthday and I didn't tell anyone. My father, because 'men don't remember things like birthdays and anniversary dates', didn't remember, and although we all just celebrated Gaspar's birthday two days prior, not a single 'well wishes' for my 16th birthday.

Eventually Satan and my three brothers would move with us into the country, into the new house. Our ages now 16, 9, 6, and 2.

Here is the first and only place I saw Satan make something close to a 'friend'. In my innocent eye, I thought Satan, like I had been in Wichita Falls, Texas, was tired of being lonely. If this was the last place they were to live, she surely would want to make friends. But I was wrong. She stuck her nose up to the neighbors, particularly other Mexican families, who were few and far between. She loved to call white people, white trash, but the way she hated her own Mexican community was pure racism and self-hate. She thought them lower than whatever 'white trash' was and did not want to me associated. She didn't make friends with other parents of kids, and soon, she would start teaching and never make friends with the coworkers.

The one person I thought was her friend was another manipulation. I mention her friend history to make the claim that she doesn't view people as relationships, but as tools, means to an end for her self-centered lifestyle. She was never friends with this person and here's why I think so;

Hermes got a job at the town hospital, as a physician assistant. The town population was 823 in 2000, and he became a favorite caretaker. Satan was a jealous wife and even his patients made her green, so it's not a stretch to say, Satan would be envious of my father's nurse. Hermes slept 7-8 hours in the day and worked with his nurse 10-12 hours, 24 hours if the 'on-call' day was busy.

Satan was not making a friend, she was grasping for any amount of control over a woman who was closer to Hermes than she was. His nurse was also nicer, funnier, and overall optimistic; people enjoyed being around her. And in true, abusive, controlling behavior, Satan kept her enemies closer. Satan constantly called this woman "dumb blond" and "stupid white woman," to her face, but then she would laugh about it and call her "girlfriend".

As per usual, since a new school year was

coming in, a new barrage of insults would be hurled at me to continue her 'breakdown/build up' exercise. I was excited to join the choir here, after having been taken out of the ensemble and concerts in Texas for a punishment. I would dance around my room to Britney, Destiny's Child, and Christina Aguilera. I would be half-enjoying myself and half-scared Satan would swing the door open while I was in a dance move or enjoying a favorite song, to be humiliated with feminine names like 'Tykeria' (Tyriel+Shakira) or 'Spastic hips'.

My grandmother (Hermes' mother) taught me some hand sewing techniques and I had made a pillow and boxers. Satan would call me Buffalo Bill, the killer from Silence of the Lambs, whom sewed and had that dick between the legs scene. She would ask me if I was doing that pose in the mirror while I sewed and modeled the stance when fashion was mentioned; just mean for mean sake.

I had two years left of high school and made a small group of friends here. I don't know how other queer 'past-friendship' experiences occurred, but my best friend in North Dakota came out gay; my best male friend in San Angelo, Texas came out gay, and my best friend here would eventually come out as gay.

My friend here, in Long Prairie, tried to come out to me in our senior year. I still believed gay people were going to hell, and so did he, but I told him, "Me and you are good people. We are not going to hell, so we can't be gay." And he agreed, but confessed to me that he had to imagine males when masturbating, and I told me (in my own delusion), "All guys do that. We just don't talk about it." I truly believed that, and he truly believed me and so he didn't come out that year.

Chapter 12 – Nursing Needs

There would be a break from Satan.

I took my SAT's (an irrelevant IQ test, used to group people for college acceptance) and I did very well, but my friend did not do well, and we decided to attend a community college that didn't care about SAT scores. We got a college owned apartment in Brainerd.

I was still under the direction of my parents, but since I did not know what I wanted to do, the study of 'generals' was the goal; going to school for the purpose of going to school. The actually goal was to find out what I wanted to really study by the end of the two years, get an associate's degree and transfer to a bigger college.

I, however, took this as an opportunity to breathe, and once off Satan's leash, I was ready to run, at least walk....cautiously. I acclimated fairly quickly to the idea that Satan was not hiding around the corner or waiting to burst open my bedroom door. My door could close and had a lock on it!

My friend and I lived in a 4 bedroom apartment with two other students. The whole complex was a party palace. Drinking and drugs were everywhere. I dabbled in smoking marijuana but avoided most drugs because of stigmas. I'd been given a nugget of weed I didn't know how to 'clean' or smoke, so I stashed it in my underwear drawer and forgot about it. Except for alcohol, alcohol was legal and my parents drank, so it seemed safer than other party avenues.

Drinking would become a life-changing challenge but that's jumping ahead. A healthier life-changing event would occur first in my classes.

I did manage to attend school while enjoying a social life and in two of my classes I met my first queer people. I of course met other queer people in the multiple places I lived or even on television but I didn't know any of them personally. In my English and Physical Education class, both my teachers were lesbians. Lesbians married to each other, but more important than lesbians, they were kind, nice, smart people. The English teacher, in particular, was the nicest person I had ever met (even now! Although I may have heighten the memories of her optimism.) At the time the only other lesbians pointed out to me, by Satan, were hell-bound. The wires in my head frayed at the thought of a god punishing this kind lady to hell, simply because she was married to another nice lady. Especially, when the same god would welcome Satan into heaven.

This disconnect broke my belief in a god, AND helped me realize, "I'm gay!" I came out to myself right away, like a light switch, I even came out to my best friend and some neighbors; not yet to my parents.

I still held all my bigoted views. Just because I had discovered that queers were not going to hell, didn't mean I suddenly started loving myself and finding acceptance. Hell was not nearly as much of a threat as Satan was.

I still carried all of my self-doubt and anxieties and I thought I had to be a 'socially acceptable' gay, a 'straight coded and quiet about my homosexuality' gay; a definition I made up based on my insecurities with femininity, and what my parents considered acceptable. I could never be one of those flamboyant gays, shoving their queerness in people's faces; I was, in general, terrified Satan would find out and this would be another disappointment. I feared the punishment that would fall on me for being gay but I dreaded the disappointment and shame I was to bring on the family.

My best friend also came out to himself and his family but religiously he struggled. However, scholarly he succeeded. We didn't hang out much after that, I went into party mode and he went on to fulfill his two years and graduate further, get a nice job, house, and husband. They live with adopted children in a small city and I'm happy he got his goal. My own college adventure, though, would go sideways.

I had a laptop from school, and to help find other gays, I went on the internet. The internet was another world Satan had not allow me on prior. She didn't know how to work it well, being it was fairly new and not as user friendly, so she didn't want me to learn it either. Now it was at my fingertips. I heard about a gay website from another student (Google was not a thing yet.) I logged into Gay.com; back then it was free, and I made an account.

I thought, I was an ugly silly straw of a person,

but on the internet I was a fresh young twink, and older men, in particular, flocked. All these sexually driven men were now ready to educate me on all the sex things my parents didn't. I was 18 with hormones ready to run and finally my attraction was being affirmed by others. Thankfully, either Gay.com was too new and not populated or Brainerd didn't have any gay members on the site, but the closest people I found attractive, were hours away. I say 'thankfully' because with my lack of self-control, I didn't need to discover sex at that time. But, boy, did I try!

I was on the internet a lot, but then one, unfortunate, Thanksgiving, the complex was broken into and appliances were stolen all over multiple apartments, including my laptop. I started using the computer lobby at the school to talk with guys because the school was only a block away, but it had a curfew. I discovered if I was in the lobby before the curfew, I could leave whenever with the doors locking behind me. This became my new routine.

I also loved plants and would walk through the horticultural wing to get home and in a naïve, entitled fashion, when I saw a plant wilting I brought it home and took care of it. Sounds innocent enough, but I did it like 10 times. Sometimes I would return the plants when they were doing better, but I would put them in different spots around the school, where they would get watered with others of its kind by the janitors.

A wild party in multiple apartments caught the attention of the police and when they arrived to meet the complaints they had previous complaints about stolen plants from the school.

I was discovered as the plant thief! The plants belonged to the school, the school belonged to the state, so I was facing a bigger crime than I understood. The school kicked me out, Hermes paid for a well-known lawyer to talk me out of the crime, and I was back home with Satan.

I didn't want to lie, to myself or them, so I came out within an hour of coming back home. It, naturally, led to an argument, with Satan using the f-slur for gays and telling me I had just ruined my life and I might as well inject myself with AIDS. She even, accusingly, asked me if I sexually abused my brothers. She went on to say, nobody would love me, "Not real love" and she talked about her pride and how she didn't want to have to move again. At the end of the night she demanded I don't tell anymore people, get back in the closet, and don't embarrass my brothers while they finished their schooling. Hermes, who was also devastated to watch the 'manliness' leave his dreams for me, decided to put the 'gay issue' on the back burner while we dealt with the school, court stuff, and the pot I still had that Satan would find after digging through my things.

So now I was a crooked nose, pigeon toed, lying buffalo-bill, f-slur, girly-sinner, who was too dumb for an associate's degree, living back with my parents. Satan loved it. She got to double down all of her abuse under the guise of 'I told you so.' She told me it was obvious I needed the control and structure. She blamed my wild streak for 'turning' me gay and thought it could be reversed, converted back.

Satan didn't understand the 'cruel world' she thought was outside our house ready to tear me apart for being gay, was actually her. She was the bully she was warning me about, and was either to abused herself to realize that, or she over exaggerating the cruelty to

87

prove a point, but no one has ever treated me consistently less than, for being gay, as she as.

I was still 18, turning 19, and my youngest brother, Balthasar, just turned 5. When he started attending school, Satan also started teaching so she could protect/watch him and her other sons in school. Her control was out of control. While she was away, my schedule was filled with 'straight' lessons in the form of physical, mental, and spiritual labor.

Physically; I had all my house cleaning duties back (beds, floors, dishes, etc.) plus new farm duties. I only lived in Long Prairie for two years prior to college, and the farm was being built for most of that time, so previously I didn't have any farm chores.

My father kept his promises to Satan and the farm was a good arm's length away. It was still visible from the house, but tightly tucked on the other side of a small hill. My job was to put in a white picket fence for Satan, with the punishment of doing so by a manual posthole digger. She wanted it around the house; a big back yard, long ass front yard, including the 50 yard drive way, with 4 gates on each side big enough for a tractor. I don't know what kind of school she thought I went to, or what kind of work I did around the trailer park, but I hadn't the slightest clue what to do.

Hermes would say, "Don't think of it as punishment, you're just helping out around the farm!" To me feeding and cleaning the cows was helping out, helping build a chicken coop (inside and out) and pheasant coop, taming and riding a horse, picking rocks (oh so many rocks!) was helping out-maintenance type things and things done WITH the person who wants it done. Satan wanted a border around her house, to separate it from the farm and she wanted it to be fancy so passer-byers would complement her. Nobody was going to help me build the fence, this wasn't help, this was a job, and after explaining my point Hermes agreed and paid me to do it.

I pounded the ground out that summer/fall with just my posthole digger all around that plot of land, placing white beams every 6 feet with corner and gate posts 6 feet down. I dug holes that could fit three bodies worth just to remove an oddly placed rock in a designated pole spot. I had Jesus holes from the mighty blisters popped in my hands that I wrapped up to continue getting the job done. I staggered white planks back and forth to create Satan's desired aesthetic, installed the gates, and finished.

Meanwhile, I would hear arguments revolving around how much I was to get paid, "You don't get paid for punishments. You're too soft. He's manipulating you," Satan would say to Hermes. Eventually, I got paid a $1 a post, about $120, and any time that fence was brought up Satan would remind me I got paid for that, and Hermes would proudly proclaim it as if it was some sort of accomplishment. That fence, and the barn, were torn down the second they left that house when someone else moved in, to open up the land.

Mentally; my punishment continued in lesson plans and isolation. Satan would have me sit at the dinner table and write over and over again, 'Homosexuality is a sin and I am a sinner. I ask God for forgiveness,' and 'I am attracted to women. I want to find a woman to marry.' I had not mentioned my separation from religion but regardless Satan knew she could not force me to pray, but she could watch me write and as a teacher this was her go to lesson plan.

In accordance with wanting me to date women, women were the only humans allowed over to the house. My best friend was blamed for putting the idea of gay in my mind and Satan didn't want him around the kids anymore. I had no door, no music, no phone, and no internet access. I was learning to shop for myself and bought 'funky' tees that she threw away for being 'too loud'. Cellphones and the internet were just booming so it wasn't super noticeable not having them, but I wanted to check my Gay.com.

I snuck on the home computer and checked my account. I sent some messages and all though I thought I logged out, I did not. Satan discovered the page later that day along with my profile pics, including a dick pick! Her response was to smile and express, "Wow, you are a lot bigger than I remember." If she considered me her son I would say, what an incestual pervert, but she doesn't so; what a just normal pervert.

Spiritually; Satan's punishment manifested as church attendance and visiting the priest afterhours. Church was an actual escape from the house and it was nice to sit and go in my imagination. With the priest alone, a different vibe filled the room, maybe it was the topic. We talked like a therapist would, about college and the gay website. He was very intrigued about what and how far I had been with another guy and our conversations stayed 'professional.' I didn't know I could or should talk about Satan, because she had sent me there, so I didn't ever trust him as a helper. My help came in the form of most gay men's help at this age; women.

It was October 31st, Satan I had another argument and she had backhanded me with her wedding ring hand leaving a gouge in my cheek that Hermes was stitching up on the couch. I wanted to go to a party that evening and Satan heard my gay friend would be there and was not allowing it. After I got stitched up below my right eye, I went upstairs to bed. I put a pillow-dummy in my bed and snuck out the window, off the roof, and through the field. I ran to the neighbor's house, called a friend, got a ride and went to that party. The stitches were a hit.

While talking to two friends there, whom happen to be women, I found out they were moving the very next day to St. Paul. They were looking for one more roommate but they were going to move either way. I jumped on the opportunity and with the little money I had left over, from working in college and the fence job, I moved to the Twin Cities November 1st.

Chapter 13 – Quaint Quality

I got a couple phone calls when Satan noticed I left but I didn't answer them. I never got a phone call from Hermes about it, so I do wonder what she told him for him not to worry. Later on when talking to him about it, he didn't know what time or situation I was referring to. He was checked out.

I was starting from scratch, but in the city, my freedom and explorative side came out again. I started journaling, mainly to keep phone numbers of the people I met as I didn't have a cell phone. I was going on internet dates and finding the hot spots, and as a gay I eventually ended up at the Gay 90's, a popular dance club. Here as a wall flower, I would meet my two best friends, Preah Ko and Preah Keo. This would be a healthy petri dish for growth and finally I could start finding myself again after 14 years.

We frolicked through the city. Preah Ko found beauty in everything and he taught me to take time to look at myself in the mirror and appreciate myself. He quieted my negative comments and compared me to fashion models and actors. It's not that he replaced Satan's words but he gave me another perspective from which to view myself. My nose didn't have to be 'big and crooked', it was 'strong and commanding.' My big ears weren't "radar plates", they were elflike and cool. I was tall enough, strong enough, good enough to be his friend, and he was more than nice to me about it.

The three of us explored our genders and fashion, and we loved to dance. We went dancing almost every night of the week and created the newest craziest fashions, we were the lesser known club kids of Minneapolis. I would cut up literal fishing net and get caught in it, or sew shaggy bathroom mats into my jeans. Belts on belts and belts everywhere. Every shirt could be a crop top and every pant a daisy duke.

My friends taught me love doesn't need to come with pain. There were many a drunk, drugged up nights we would be sharing personal stories of our upbringing and I would mention Satan's actions as an understanding to someone else's situation. Friends would stop me and say, "that's actually not okay. That's abuse." I laughed it off the first twenty times but then I would eventually have to start taking it seriously.

They gave me the encouragement and time to discover who I was, as they were doing. They wanted me to be the best version of myself, whatever that was. I am humbly grateful to my friends, Preah Ko in particular [You are a magical positive ray of sunshine, radiating compassion on this planet.] Today in 2022, I have just barely started calling myself open-minded and still have to work through my indoctrinated bigotry, but I see beyond myself now, past my privileges, and that's a gift I can't thank my friends enough for.

I'm not saying my parents should have been friends; Satan didn't want to be, and Hermes was absent, but moving forward they would never be friends even though I was no longer a child. I understand that change between child and individual can be hard for parents, and training wheels can be healthy and helpful. But realizing my parents had plans for me as a child that never fruited made them constantly view me as a child and never let them see the individual I was becoming. Also they closed their senses off to getting to know me, I was a gay guy having gay sex and gay drugs in the gay city. I was told not to tell them, or my brother's, about anything gay related, even my work at a 'girl's' clothing store was gay to them. I didn't know what made something 'gay', so I didn't talk to them about work, clubs, or friends, or hobbies.

I left Saint Paul to get deeper into Minneapolis. This is where I spent all my time and even after moving away for a short period I would buzz around this city living in several different homes from a pent house to a closet and nearly everything in between; a loft, an apartment, a studio, the empty house of a lottery winner, my car, downtown, uptown, rooftop, etc.

I have carried over 50 jobs to date from tutor to business owner; I've done serving, gophering, auctioning, maintenance, design, marketing, accounting, customer service, phone operating, banking, managing, DJing, etc. Just a brief list I may expand upon in a later memoir.

Whilst in and out of jobs I was starting to drink and do drugs pretty heavily. I partied Wednesday night to Monday night, only taking Tuesday off to recover. I was still in my 20's and used that as an excuse to keep going, but it was growing into a problem.

When a queer child comes from a house that isn't affirming in their person; they are often stunted in their personal growth. It doesn't change or reform; it shuts down and lets the survival mode take over. While other cis-het children fit the blue print of how to raise a child, queer children often need to create a new path with their guardians and if those guardians are not willing to help, that path can start late (and be dangerous) in life (in comparison to our cis-het brothers and sisters). These queer children are more likely to be abandoned by their families (either they leave or get kicked out) and become part of the houseless youth. These queer houseless are more likely to be victimized and turn to illegal sex work for money and get into drugs because of their environment.

According to the worldpopulationreview.com, the United States has the 3rd highest houseless population percentage, as of 2022, (and of the top three - USA is the only one predicted to continue growing) and it could be broken down as:

.02% of Americans are houseless – That's about 570,000 people unevenly distributed across the country and of this number about 16% are youth. I tried to find the smallest percentages I could so people wouldn't think I'm fudging numbers, but some numbers show up to 40% youth, because of hard to track ever-changing numbers, and the uneven distribution.

We should be upset about any number of our members living without houses, not out of pity, but disappointment in our government laws and care. Especially our kids, and if 35,000 houseless youth doesn't sound like a lot, the number is most likely higher because of the dangerous death rate, lying on the census (a prideful kid might not consider themselves houseless – I didn't even when living out of my car) and if they survive the streets, they age out of the youth bracket.

At 19, I was not kicked out of my house, I had been sent to college and was very privileged; I was white-passing, cis-passing, hetero-passing, economically stable and all though I didn't believe I was attractive, at minimum, I was average looking. Keeping in mind I was actually Spanish, raised in a Mexican house hold, Gay, Trans, Ace, and poor once off my parents income-but I still had my privileges from society, outside my bubble. It would take me sometime to understand that, but it was relevant here.

Besides drugs and alcohol, I also dated a lot. I had about 8 boyfriends by 22. Satan, simple because I was gay, thought I was bending over for every hole post. I was, actually, afraid of sex because after coming out, Satan had homophobically told me, "f-(gay) sex makes your insides fall out of your ass". I didn't know if that was true or not and Hermes, as a medical profession, just said, "Yeah, that could happen."

I messed around with guys, nothing to intense, but my boyfriends wanted to have sex and I told each one of them to give me time, at least '3 months' and then we could do it. But like clockwork at 3 months we would get into an argument and the relationship would dissolve. It took me years after to realize I was subconsciously preventing sex. I, eventually, at 22, had sex with a hot yogi bartender friend, not a boyfriend, and absolutely hated it. He didn't know I hated it, I was very good at pretending to enjoy situations I didn't care for.

After finally having sex and not liking it I wondered what all the hype was about. I made it a goal to 'like' sex, there are many different penises and many different ways to sex them so I shouldn't let one bad session determine the overall experience.

Sexually I exploded, which is easy to do in the gay world. I went to sex parties, both planned and spontaneous, tried bondage, rope, role-play, three-somes, cuckholding, piss play, rubber, leather, fur, cameras, worship, etc. None of it was appealing to me, but I kept trying to find out why there was nothing I enjoyed, and what I was doing wrong. I wouldn't find the label and community of Asexuals for a while longer and I would continue to put myself in dangerous misguided situations to both get attention and fit in.

Also around this time Bastet, my bio-mom, had reached out to my father. She had found religion and was calling to make amends on people she had hurt throughout her life. When I say amends, I mean doing the least you could do by calling someone and saying 'I'm sorry' without proving you're sorry or actually doing anything to amend the hurt. She, despite calling to 'amend', was also secretly calling to ask Hermes if he would get back together with her. Along with her apology came a confession of long lasting love and an open invitation to get back together. Hermes was not about to do that, both because he didn't want to go back with her, and because he didn't want to leave the family he created-even if he was not happy. He was not about to add ANOTHER divorce to his relationship resume; the blasphemy. He denied her offer and before they got off the phone she asked for my number and continued her apology tour.

When she called me, I gave her the "I forgive you," she was looking for so she could cross me off her list. When she pushed to get to know me, I told her I was gay, and she let me know that was okay because she "hates the sin, not the sinner." But apparently the sin kept her away because she didn't call back for another five years and it wouldn't be because she picked up the phone. Her daughter, my half –sister, Parvati, would eventually find me on Facebook, but that's another adventure.

During one beautiful boyfriend, I was failing at a job, drinking lots, and falling behind on finances. I was dating an inspirational, graduated, service worker and I, with my low self-image, could not keep up with him. But I had a plan.

I was ready to start college again and looked into the idea. I knew that I would not be able to concentrate with my wild, party life calling to me right outside the door, so I made the very hard decision to stop the check-to-check grind and leave the city (and my boyfriend.) I had to work on myself and be a better me, whatever that meant. Coincidentally, the change also happened three months into this relationship so maybe I was also feeling the need to flee.

I ran to Alexandria, Minnesota. A community college specialized in law enforcement that was about a forty minute drive from Long Prairie, and a two hour drive from the cities. I reconnected with some high school friends and directed my studies towards business after having become a manager at a couple clothing stores in the Mall of America.

Here I lived in another basement situation, with three other quickly rotating students, mostly, future police officers. I didn't drop, but lulled my drinking habit to the VFW. I managed to get a boyfriend in the two years of schooling there with another server at the Perkins I worked at. I was doing well in school while more self-motivated.

Near the end of my school time, the landlord, of the basement, died and I had to move out. I moved to my parent's house to finish out the year and got a heavy dose of the evil I had escaped from before.

Chapter 14 – Tiny Trip

Living at home was the last thing I wanted to do, but it was only supposed to be for a month and then I would transfer to a university in the cities. Mine and my brother's ages were 24, 17, 14 and 10. Everyone was still at home, but the house was empty most of the time with everyone at school and work. And when we were together Satan was normally in front of the others. Her attitude was always fowl but we were rarely alone for her to outright belittle me.

This was proof to me that she was conscious of what she was doing. She was poking me in the sides and pinching my arms when no one was watching, still at this age. She only used gay slurs when my brothers were not around because she didn't want them to know I was gay, and she would say things like, "I can be artistic, too, like you, even though we are not blood," but still lied to my half-brothers about our relationship. Then when the rest of the family entered the room the insults continued just more obscure, "are you ready to date a girl?" "Have you finished getting sin out of your system yet?" "You're your dad's son." Vague enough comments to psychologically insult me without calling me out.

I was making plans to move in with my boyfriend at the time, in the cities and we were looking for places to live. Satan didn't know this and I would tell her I was working at Perkins (in Alexandria), but instead we would go apartment hunting. Satan said she was innocently coming into buy some muffins for Hermes when she found out I wasn't working. She was appalled and offended by the lie, which is fair, but instead of coming to me like an adult and saying her feelings and letting me say mine; she went to my room while I was out and prepared for a reveal.

We got into another big argument-when I say argument, I called Satan a 'bitch' once when I was 10, under my breath. I wasn't calling her names or accusing her of anything, other than being nosey. I wasn't throwing things or pushing, poking, etc. She on the other hand was destroying my personal items, while spitting and throwing things at me. She called me untrustworthy and devilish (she traded the term 'gay' with 'sinning' so she could say it freely in front of her sons). I don't know if this is what offended her most or

106

if she just needed something of 'substance' to cling to but she was yelling that I had let my boyfriend know our address and he had pulled into the driveway (to pick me up) while everyone was gone. When I asked why she thought he was a gay, let alone my boyfriend, she pulled my journal from behind her back and pointed to the part where we started dating. She became irate because she caught me in 'another lie' and thought her 43 year old actions appropriate. She began ripping up my journal and hitting me with it. She threw cds and broke a desk lamp trying to chuck it at me but it was still plugged in, which made her angrier and she grabbed my stereo and hurled that instead. Anything under her roof was ammo, whether it was in my luggage bag, or not, didn't matter. In the end, the biggest lost was that she kept the rest of the journal with her; the phone numbers I collected from my time in the city.

My boyfriend let me stay at his apartment for the remaining of college until we were ready to leave.

I transferred my serving job to a Perkins in the city and moved to Minneapolis. My boyfriend couldn't handle my parental drama OR my own residual, unpacked drama and backed away; at first slowly, then abruptly. I hold nothing against him or any of my exes. I think we all had a lot of childhood grievances to acknowledge but I can't speak for them.

This is the power of abuse, I hated Satan and still felt like I had to love her. If she had asked for help for the smallest thing I would have returned to her, without question. I still called the house and said 'I love you', and wished her 'happy birthday' every year, like we sons were REQUIRED to do.

It made it all meaningless to me; does she merely need to hear the words 'happy birthday' or 'I love you' or did she actually want me to mean it? Meanwhile, my birthday is getting forgotten every other year to keep me on my toes.

I also still thought what my parents had was healthy. I wanted to get married and have kids just like them...just like them. I carried abusive tantrums into my relationships and manipulated them, consciously. I did not know how to love, or what real love was. I wasn't sure if I loved Satan, I just went through the motions. I still wondered why my father didn't divorce

108

her, because he was also now clearly unhappy. But I was out of the house and he knew how I felt.

Unfortunately, my brothers had no idea how I felt. I couldn't talk to them about dating, clubs, any of life's fun firsts or 'gay' things, in general. I couldn't talk to them about my bio-mom or my step-mom, or a new family that came out of the wood work when my half-sister found me.

As my brothers hit the age of 18, one by one, I told them the truth and apologized for the lies. I wanted to get closer with them and start building a relationship, EACH TIME.

I had already been labeled a black sheep by then and they were persuaded to move in the opposite direction when looking for a college, they all attended school on the North Dakota border. We never grew close, but the idea of family loyalty was soo strong, Gaspar named his first born after me, as if I was already dead and gone.

Chapter 15 – Hardy Har

I memorized Preah Ko's number and through him got a few other number's back. The rest I had to chalk up to a 'Satanic panic' loss.

I finally got a cell phone and Hermes insisted that I call every week, but he was never there to answer the phone and it became once a month. Over the years I distanced myself even more, only going home for two to three holidays per year.

I stopped partying with drugs, other than weed and alcohol, but the weed and alcohol were pretty constant. I was still living paycheck to paycheck and didn't pick up college right away; I had to pay off the loans from the Alexandria school.

One drunken night walking out of the bar, I ran into an ex-boyfriend, Cu Chulainn. We dated when I was 20. 2004 ~ I was with Preah Ko at the same bar and we were talking about dating tips and I wanted to show Preah Ko how to confidently walk up to a guy and say 'hi.' I saw Cu Chulainn at a pool table playing a game. He was tall, dark and handsome, with a masculine swagger. He wore a Texas long-horn shirt and was winning. I went over to him, complimented him on his shirt and eyes. He had a nervous big smile and said, "thank you," and we exchanged numbers. Cu Chulainn had the cutest blue pickup truck he would grind into the road and he was a very attentive boyfriend. He was a GREAT boyfriend at the time but his 3 months were up and, typical me, I cut it off, calling him to clingy and not old enough to go to the bar with me (I had just turned 21), arbitrary complaints disguising my own insecurities.

But here he was, seven years later, outside the SAME bar; he was passing by at 27 and I was stumbling out of it at 28. We exchanged numbers again, and after a few dates we started dating again and we dated for seven years. He was my longest boyfriend and I bothered the crap out of him to get married, but he hated the idea of marriage (and its history). I grew to agree with him. It took a while to question my views on marriage and how it, as any tool, can be wielded in good and bad ways. Religiously, marriage is a transaction, often making one person (usually a woman) the property being transacted. Kids, at 18, rush into marriages to get around religious barriers for sex and religion can cement couples into an unhealthy marriage; undeveloped personalities, shame on divorce, unbalanced roles, financial traps, etc. Governmentally, it aligns couples as a unit, combining money and rights. Very simplistic explanations of my thought process, but nonetheless, we decided not to get married.

One of the best gifts Cu Chulainn gave me was the ability to research things. I was still having sex, and not liking it, but Cu Chulainn and I had an open door for conversation about nearly everything and he was patient. I went online and simple asked, "Why don't I like sex?" There were many reasons why people don't care for sex; trauma, anxiety, lack of attraction. Some of those I could eliminate, I was attracted to Cu Chulainn; and some didn't make sense, maybe I was carrying abuse from my past.

Surely, I had anxiety but (as of 2022) 19.1% of Americans have anxiety and more than that have 'trauma' and they're still enjoying sex. At age 30, I finally found the term 'Asexual' - a community of people who have none, or very little, attraction to sex. There is a massive spectrum for this community and itself could be a book 10xbigger than this- the basic definition I gave works for me but not every Ace person.

I realized it didn't matter how or why. If I wasn't attracted to sex, whether it be nature or nurture; I wasn't attracted to sex.

I was Asexual and I was excited to have a community. Cu Chulainn and I trialed and errored different styles of relationship, and we agreed on an amazing balance.

At 33, my drinking was still out of control and I was blacking out, almost all the time. I was escaping from the pain of anxiety, and excused it into alcoholism. I was drinking a handle every day, no matter where I was; home, work, park, wherever and everywhere with a bottle stowed away in my backpack. Medically, the drink was eating away the lining of my stomach and blocking me from absorbing the proper nutrients. This in turn weakened by spinal cord and pressed it against my nerves. My left leg was going numb and, literally, no longer able to move.

Instead of the heavy drinking for over a decade, I blamed it on a new 'sit-down' job I got, after getting out of serving for also a decade. Eventually, one day at work, I keeled over in pain and could not get back up and Cu Chulainn took me to the hospital where we discovered the problem. The doctors told me I should have been dead by now and they were astounded I made it as far as I had. They gave me less than a week to live, as I had internal bleeding, from my stomach. I had to learn to put down the bottle, quick.

It was hard to do, and I was very sad to leave the bar and stop dancing, but I knew if I kept drinking I would also not be able to dance (and as it was I couldn't dance anyway). I loved life (I love life) and I had to stop this self-harm.

Long story, short, I did, but the hardest part was going to my brother's wedding. My family normalized drinking, and they didn't have a hint of the struggle I had went through and was in. It started out as a 'gay hobby' (partying at bars) and since my parents didn't want to hear about that, when it evolved into a health problem it was still blurred with 'gayness' so it was another topic lost to their denial. If I would have died then, they, most likely, would have blamed Cu Chulainn and never questioned themselves.

I, unfortunately, did give in to drinking during Gaspar's wedding. It was fine, beside the guilt, and it was the last a time I drank booze. Coincidentally, as a gift to the wedding party, Gaspar gave us brothers flasks with his wedding date engraved on it. So I have a reminder of my last drop drank in the form of a hidden coat swig.

Once I stopped drinking I found my joy for life to blossom even more. I was able to write and draw again; two talents that I wanted to do but physically could not because of the shaking of my hands. I was even able to go to the bar and dance; the feeling in my leg came back 98%. I am, highly fortunate, to have minimal drinking urges. I drank because I liked to drink, and now that I saw it was hurting me, I didn't care for it as much anymore and it was easy to let go (maybe a metaphor for Satan also).

One sober afternoon after a nap, I woke up to find Cu Chulainn huffing over a wooden puzzle box. He asked for my help and I gave it to me. It was a pretty decorative cube with lots of meticulous designs on it, but nothing to open. I handed it back and he suggested we do it together. He discovered a sliding piece and I took over from their and managed to defeat the puzzle. Inside was a scroll and on it written in gold leaf lettering was a short question, 'Will you Marry me?' In another hidden drawer was a gold ring. I said yes right away but sat, flabbergasted for thirty minutes. I was soo happily surprised, because I thought it was already decided we were not to get married. When we first started dating, gays weren't allowed to get married and since the law change we had talked it out of our future, out of the question.

Now it was happening. I thought I was dreaming. Cu Chulainn and I are happily married today and strong as ever. He told me later he wanted to marry me because after the hospital scare he didn't want my family to be able to make decisions on my behalf. I had never known a love that proved itself more than it announced itself; a love that can be healthy.

Cu Chulainn and I focused on what our goal was. We knew we were a good team; we took a three month bike trip to the Grand Canyon and for the most

116

part succeeded. We both were tired of working for other people and wanted more free time and we focused on entrepreneuring and after a few stumbles we built a career and started working together, out of our apartment.

Chapter 16 – Gone Gay

Before our wedding, I began to research my mental struggles. I researched the Cinderella effect, I researched, racism, and abuse (mainly abuse on women to try and understand Satan), I researched POC experiences and Mexican struggles in the United States. I was starting to understand myself better and was hoping to understand Satan and why she was the monster I believed her to be.

Satan grew up in Corpus Christi, Texas. Her family was on the low income branch and her, and her six brothers and sisters (three each), lived in a small house. During the summers they would get sent to a strawberry patch in Minnesota and gather bundles. Satan liked basketball in school but said she was bullied by everyone, especially the other girls. She said she hadn't any high school friends but did talk about a friend with 'hair down to her feet', so maybe that came after high school. When I was about 7, we went to see her hometown, and she visited her friend, by herself and came back angry and never wanted to come to Corpus Christi again. We did go back to see her parents, but her friend, 'Flora' with the long hair, was never mentioned again.

Satan was in an abusive relationship before she met Hermes, but 'abusive' is the only description I heard, and if you ask me, any relationship she is in could be described that way, sooo.

I can understand a fraction of the toll and aggravation she endured as a Mexican in a white dominated population. I, as a third party, witnessed her interaction with many people and recognized blatant racism and sexism towards her.

I don't need to understand any of that to know that when I was growing up, she was with, and with us she was NO LONGER being abused from a past relationship. She had the finances she dreamed of, she lived in a safe place, no one in the house was being racist or sexist to her in a way she didn't think was appropriate (I, technically, think we were all racist/ sexist etc. but blind to the internal critique). She didn't have to work and she had the kids/family she wanted.

Some people are just mean, I guess, and I hate to think that because a.) I don't think there are inherently 'bad' people, just bad actions and b.) I think anyone can change – if they, themselves, want to. I had changed, multiple times over trying to find a version that wouldn't annoy her, but I don't think Satan wanted to change. I think she felt entitled to her position and disposition based off her childhood experiences and ironically went on to destroy my childhood; repeating the cycle. Maybe I would have repeated the cycle had I not taken the time to understand myself before starting another generation with my broken parts.

I was very happy with my progression and on a holiday visit to my parent's house, I wanted to have a serious conversation and address my abusive upbringing with Satan in an educated, understanding, calm way. I knew she was prone to outrages, so it would take a subconscious prepping and a gentle tone.

Too late! The bottles were open and she and Hermes were sloshed around a table and we were all arguing. Hermes, whom rarely cries (how unmanly), was angrily crying because he was tired of me bringing up my bio-mom, his ex-wife, Bastet; and that family.

He wanted it to be erased and never brought up again. This is why it's soo hard to find answers about the first five years of my life; Hermes put that history in a box and lit it on fire. He pounded the table and went to bed upset.

Satan was also crying, but in a weird turn of events, she was apologizing for being a bad mother. She was admitting to letting her aggression out on me, and pointing her harshness at me. She didn't call it abuse, she called it 'being mean' but it was some form of acknowledgement.

I also cried that night, out of confusion/anger/relief/sadness, but in the morning, it was all taken back. She denied remembering and saying any of it. I was being gas lit, obviously, and was furious. Cu Chulainn and I went home and I revalued my relationship goals with Satan.

I put that conversation aside for over a year. I had brought it up to Hermes and he shrugged it off as me lying. It was frustrating to have, at most, an hour of conversation with my father every month only to have Satan defend herself for the rest of the month. Hermes and I had been making dates in the town between our homes to attempt to get to know each other better. I still wanted to make my parents proud so I invited Hermes and Satan to Cu Chulainn and I's wedding party. We actually got married quietly at a restaurant with a small group of witnesses but I invited them to the wedding party.

The wedding party was amazing; a beautiful outdoor day with music (I chose every song) and food (fantastic hor'dourve like treats) and most spectacularly, I decorated seventeen mannequins to be art pieces placed around the pavilion. My theme was a wedding being held in Pompeii the moment of the eruption. The attendants were frozen in time!

I created an officiant, three best men and three best women, a ring-bearer and flower girl, a decorative center piece, and three dancers on a grassy dance floor, and four audience members. I resculpted, painted and decorated the statues with vines, leaves, and flowers as if Mother Nature was bringing life back into their bodies- A wedding frozen throughout time; a truly never ending love.

I sent Satan a text saying (actual text message): *'Hi [Satan], it's been two years since my confrontation of your child raising choices. I left it up to you to reach out and Dad has let me know your concerns that have been preventing you from continuing and that's totally a valid decision, I'm not trying to rush or even suggest it as a possibility, you do what is best for yourself. That being said, I'm not comfortable with faking a relationship. Our side dialogue is fine, but I find, that I tell you happy birthday or mother's day etc. because you request it. That's hollow to me and I feel like it's hollow to you. Because of this, I would like no gifts for gift holidays and I'm not buying gifts for you either. Dad also mentioned [Gaspar's] concern for gifts at Christmas because of [his new son]. Soo, I was thinking, maybe as a family we could plan an event to do together rather than exchanging gifts. If we all chipped in I'm sure it would be cheaper for everyone and the time would be better spent together. And with everyone in a changing environment the transition might be easy. ALL OF THAT BEING SAID! I'm excited to see you at the ceremony [my wedding] and give you an opportunity to see me in a more natural environment, hopefully you are open to it.'*

The text was ignored but she did come to the wedding. She didn't say anything to me or Cu Chulainn, but she attended, so what more could I have asked for.

I was annoyed and angry, with myself, that I still put soo much weight in her view on me. Hermes also had goals and life achievements for me, but at least they were well defined and squashed. I was constantly grasping at straws to impress someone who would rather pinch off my skin and pour jalapeno juice in it than give me a compliment.

I carried this anger to Thanksgiving. My aunt, Coatlicue, was hosting. I went over early to help her set up after her husband had died earlier that year. It was her first big family event after his death. While setting up, she told me that Satan was there the night before, drinking, talking about me, and Satan told Coatlicue, "I will never give Tyriel the satisfaction of a conversation."

I hid my thoughts, but I was outraged Satan was freely talking about, how she wouldn't talk to me but wouldn't tell me that. What was I waiting for; a manipulative liar? I needed to drop the hope that there was anything to salvage. I stayed for dinner and listened to Satan, make fun of the weight of Coatlicue's dead husband. And I watched as not one of the family members seemed to be bothered by Satan's vulgar comments. I left that dinner, done with Satan, and quite frankly done with the enablers.

I went to the internet where I knew Satan would have to hear me and wrote the pain of my heart into a post; past notes I used to write this memoir were also used in this note and similarities can be seen. This is the actual post I uploaded to Facebook and tagged to Satan:

'**Warning personal and emotional story,*
*Trigger warning and sorry soo long***
I have always been naturally positive and optimistic. I believe a fake smile can help bring about a real one. I don't really get depressed; at most I might foresee a negative ending and try to avoid it. Because of this happy default I tend to roll with the punches and sometimes normalize (or get use to) harmful situations. I was raised by my child hood bully and was told from 5 years old how ugly and different I was from my giant Dumbo ears to my pigeon feet and literally Everything

125

in between (I was born with a right leg handicap I
painfully made myself walk as normally as possible to
not be harassed; before I got teeth braces I was called
chainsaw mouth. I have been beat by my bully (thrown
chairs. Attacked with a knife, punched slapped and
pinched. Repeatedly punished by putting Jalapeno juice
in my open wounds and [Satan] would also purposely
rip my foreskin!). Physical, Mental, and sexual abuse.
My positive (naive) outlook made me think, somehow,
this is what all kids deal with, and I accepted bizarre,
grotesque punishments without question.
I kept normalizing it until at 13 I realized, I was even
more different and less accepted than I knew. I'm a gay,
living with a bully who hates gays and is now pouring
that hate on to me in attempt to make me straight (my
bully's favorite phrase is 'if you want to bring some one
up right, you need to break them down!'...I attempted
suicide.
If this was the way someone who says, ' I love you'
treats me, than the rest of the world surely wouldn't be
as 'nice'.
I want to be clear here - I was not depressed! I was
convinced that I deserved to be treated like shit
because I was ugly, annoying, gay, and different. While

126

I was okay with being those things I was not okay with the life of torture seemingly in front of me. These people love and take care of me and they think I'm a disgusting piece of trash destined to hell so what could I possibly expect outside of the house, in the arms of the public?

I won't get into details about the suicide attempt but I was not successful... Thank goodness!!! And since then I turned 18 and ran for my life. I have met open minded, allies, Gays, Lesbians, Trans (so much of the spectrums) and grateful for the expanse of loving characters in my world!

I don't have suicidal thoughts, it's not something I struggle with. I love life and at 13 I thought there wasn't a life to love because of the weight I put in the value of my bullies words. My bully was my mom and she has gas lit and denied all of this until one drunk night she broke down and admitted she treated me 'less than' because I was not her natural born.

She's still there being a hatful bully and back to denying but I am thrilled to say after the 20th anniversary of my potential death day, she is officially out of my life!! By my doing and hard choices!!

While the initial pull of the plug was painful, it was

127

followed by overwhelming relief, astonishment and an explosion of happiness and pride. I'm finally free of you!!! I survived you!! Time to soar without the heavy load; Excited for the New Year!! (PS she's not dead. Just dead to me.)'

And that should have been the end of Satan.

Her and her sisters attacked for about three days after the post but then silence. Finally.

The business was doing great and we were quickly making thousands. It had helped pay for the wedding and was also helping Cu Chulainn and I buy a house now (another dream I thought too far out of reach). Everything was going up, up, up! And then the whole planet would come to a sudden halt and frenzy in 2020.

Chapter 17 – Zeal for Zest

In 2020, Minneapolis was the epicenter for Black Lives Matter protests held around the world. After the death and arrests of many BIPOC citizens throughout history due to the racist catalyst this country was built upon. Many of those protests, were responded to with riots; our own government attacking Americans on US land, for protesting because our government was attacking Americans on US land.

Also Covid-19, started ravaging the globe and attacking populated areas most.

It was disappointing that not a single parent, brother, cousin, aunt called to see how I was doing during this time. One might say, I could have called them, but in the farm country they have the least amount of chance of Covid reaching them and they were not dealing with soldiers rioting civilians into curfews (and I did check on their towns via the internet and knew when the first Covid case came to Long Prairie).

It was a slap in the face and an eye opener to where I really stood with this family. The family that demands an unconditional love only knows how to show it when demanded to via a birthday phone call, but when actually care is needed – out of sight out of mind.

I didn't need any of them, it's not that I didn't want any of them (besides Satan); but it was proven that I didn't NEED them to survive, or be happy.

Within the first year of Satan's absence I acquired the outstanding revelation that the self-deprecating voice in my head, was Satan's. Once I recognized that, I could actually hear the voice in my head in Satan's tone. Then I could tell it to "shut up". At first, maybe the voice would be on for about five minutes, building my anxiety, but I would remember it wasn't mine and tell it to be quiet. Then a few anxious trips later the voice would pop up and maybe this time it would talk for about three minutes before I remember to tell it to be quiet.

Before long I was able to stop the hateful voice before even a sentence could be complete. "Nope! I'm ignoring that." Now it's all but gone. I still have wild anxiety (I would love to find that switch!) but the internal hate has left and I've almost forgot what Satan sounds like.

To finish this part of the memoir on a happy note, before we get to my present day, here are some things I'm happy about since leaving:

Right before Covid-19 Cu Chulainn and I got a puppy. She is amazing and brings a smile to my face every day.

Cu Chulainn and I are still hustling to get our entrepreneur goal accomplished. He has created a lighting business with eccentric fixtures, adult websites, and clothes. I have wrote three books, so far, under a penname, a YouTube channel with Co-host CodeMan (the Vault in our Stars Productions), and started my own charity projects, like F.R.I.E.N.D.S. (a freedom from religious indoctrination- biweekly meeting for queer people who lost community because of disownment from a church.)

My morals point me towards humanity instead of trying to control humanity, like most religious values. I finally believe I am good person. I want to be a better person every day. I found that I love art and I like to help people and I refuse to let my anxiety stop me from doing either of those things.

I didn't start truly growing until I was 33, when I put the alcohol down and woke up, and I'm ready to thrive (alcohol being MY unhealthy coping prescription, not a blanket statement for stunted progress.)

My favorite Kelly Clarkson quote (she got from a friend), "Picked all my weeds but kept the flowers." I had lost quantity of family for quality of family. My husband and dog are more family than half of the blood I grew up with; in a tenth of the time. Queer people often have to learn this the hard way, but everyone could benefit from the realization that we do not choose what family we are born into, but we can leave it and choose another family if the one you were born to won't let us grow. Don't let those weeds strangle you.

I was not planning on writing about this; Satan's abuse, my anxiety, my sexual abuse; this is all embarrassing and not great lighting. That's why I'm unsure what other memoirs there would be, if any. I saved notes from Satan's abusive behavior as proof to myself, and confrontational material when it was needed.

As a writer, I thought, maybe, one day I could write a memoir but as you've read it's mainly complaints about a childhood I survived and came out better for. I said I wanted to bring light to the 'Cinderella Effect' but there was no story line of interest. But then Satan would return. Just as she had inspired me to start taking notes in the beginning of the abuse, she was back to inspire me again. This time to accumulate those notes, and give me the other reason I wanted to write this; to tell the true ending of the Bergmann family.

PART II

Pulled into the Present:

'The Big Bang'

Chapter 18 –Obligations Out

Here is where my guilt swells. I felt bad for leaving my father and brothers behind. That's how it felt to me, but in actuality I left the door open for them and no one came to it. I knew that Satan was not going to suddenly be a good person. She was a mean person and everyone around excused her mean behavior as "that's just how she is." I knew her cruel behavior would just be pointed elsewhere.

Unfortunately, no one believed me. I felt guilty for what I thought might happen but everyone else was blindsided.

If any of the Trigger Warnings from previous chapters were helpful, then please take this one most seriously: **Trigger Warning**

April Fool's day came and went and at 1:00 in the morning I got a phone call from Balthasar, my youngest brother. I didn't answer it; I assumed it was a drunk butt dial. In the morning I sent a text asking if that was the case or if there was an emergency. He texted me back, "It's an emergency. Please call" and I did. My oldest brother answered, Gaspar, and told me that Hermes had shot himself in the head last night and was dead.

I immediately suspected fowl play and began asking questions, "Who found him," "Where was the gun," He didn't know anything and told me he wasn't going into the barn, where Hermes had been shot, until after the hired cleaning crew got there and cleaned up. I told him, "You (Gaspar) should build up strength and go in there and take pictures, even if you have to do it with eyes closed. If the area gets cleaned we will lose aspects of the scene." He refused, understandably, and I didn't know how important those pictures would be. We was sobbing and I didn't want to push him.

I told him I could be there to help, and he told me I shouldn't come because Satan's sisters were already on their way and wouldn't want me to be there. I was taken aback. I asked why and he told me after the Facebook post, they (Satan's sisters, and I'm sure Satan, since she could've corrected them) didn't consider me family and my presents would be unhealthy to Satan.

I told Gaspar that was irrelevant to my father's death. I could be at a hotel or something on the outskirts of town if I was going to be considered a problem. I don't need or want to see her either, so that works for both of us. Gaspar suggested it was better if I didn't. He cut the conversation and said he would call back later.

Thirty minutes passed and he called back with a brief story of Hermes' death. He was not there, but this is what Satan told him:

It was late at night and Satan was up at the house getting ready for bed when she heard a gunshot. She knew Hermes was down in his barn and when she looked out the house window she noticed the barn light was off. She thought that was weird and went to go check on Hermes. She walked down the long dirt path to the barn and opened the door to discover him dead. She called my littlest brother who was visiting from college (he was up at the house sleeping) and he ran down to the barn and he called the police. The police and an ambulance took all three of them away and Satan and Balthasar were questioned.

I have no information from the police, at the time of writing this.

I asked how Balthasar was doing, after seeing that horrendous scene. He was very shaken up and that explained why he wasn't talking yet, but I really wanted to know his side of the story. Gaspar said he would have him call me.

I asked how Satan was. He said she was either screaming out Hermes' name to the town from her bedroom window or she was passed out from sleeping pills Balthasar was feeding her.

Despite thinking Satan and her Sisters were gross people, I was happy they were there to help my brothers. I asked Gaspar what funeral plans, or burial plans we had but he was clueless. I suggested some things off the top of my head and let him go, reassuring him I could help with anything and everything.

Chapter 19 – Yarn by the Yard

Hermes died in the early morning on the second, it was a Saturday, although April Fool's Day will forever hold a different feeling for me.

Later that Saturday, Balthasar called me. I asked where Hermes' body was and he said it was at the morgue having an autopsy done. We talked about his mental state after seeing our father's death. Balthasar was following in Hermes' footsteps through medical school to be a doctor and mentioned he had seen some brutal things before (in school) and knew how to turn off that part of his brain. He admitted though, that if Hermes' killed himself (and also witnessed bloody scenes) than maybe it wasn't as easy to compartmentalize.

His mind was still racing, like mine, trying to find out what happened. He went through the story with me, day by day of his visit:

Starting a week before, on Sunday;

Balthasar came home from out of state to enjoy his Spring break with his brothers. Our nephew, Gaspar's child, was having a birthday on Saturday and he wanted to attend.

On Monday, the three of them, Balthasar, Satan, and Hermes, went to see that same nephew and Gaspar early, planning on coming back the following Saturday.

Tuesday, the three of them travelled in the opposite direction of Gaspar's home and visited the middle child, Melchior, whom recently married and had a baby of his own. A seemingly common visit.

My parents had NEVER visited ANY of my houses out of the long list of places I have lived, since moving out 20 years ago. They didn't know the address to over half of them or my current one; yet it was common for them to go visit my other brothers-making up to three plans this particular week.

On Wednesday and Thursday, they stayed home, fished and relaxed. Balthasar mentioned that throughout the week there was an argument between Hermes and Satan:

Satan didn't like Gaspar's wife or her side of the family (surprise) and she didn't want to visit her grandchild for a second time that week, even if it was for his birthday. Satan knew Gaspar's family-in-law would be there and she didn't want to interact with them. She also didn't want to be the only people from Gaspar's side of the family attending.

Hermes argued that she was always complaining she didn't have time with her grand kids and now she was complaining it was too many times. He also pointed out, if she was worried that Gaspar doesn't have enough family representation there, then she should want to go so that he at least had them. To clarify, Satan did NOT want to go to the birthday party on Saturday, and Hermes DID.

Then on Friday morning, the argument continued with Satan saying, "I am not going!" and Hermes saying, "You don't have to go, but I am." Satan left the house mad and went shopping, and Balthasar and Hermes went to the casino. Balthasar swears on the way there and back, Hermes was in good spirits, they won money, and during the car conversation nothing brought up red flags.

When they got home Satan was back from shopping and having an early afternoon drink. She left mad to my aunt's house, Coatlicue, after she brought the topic backup and Hermes kept his stance. Balthasar and Hermes relaxed in the hot tub for a while and when they got out, Satan was getting home and she was wasted. Surprisingly, Balthasar says Hermes was not drunk, yet, but was drinking his usual beers. He would have started at noon, but they got home late from the casino around 7 PM, so he hadn't drank as much as he normally would have; it was about 10:30 when they exited the hot tub.

Balthasar said he could tell there was stress between the two, because they sat in angry silence as they finished watching a show before Balthasar excused himself to bed. He claims he didn't hear ANYTHING; no arguing, no gun shots, just silence. His bed was in the basement and out of four rooms his was the furthest one away, but, regardless, he said he heard nothing. He was only in bed for about twenty minutes before he got the phone call.

He woke up to the frantic call from Satan saying 'Hermes shot himself' and he ran, in his boxers and bare feet, down the muddy driveway and found Satan at Hermes' side apologizing.

I asked what Satan was apologizing for, and he said she was crying and hard to understand but he believes 'just about life in general.'

He continued to describe the scene, which I won't, but he mentioned Hermes was still alive. He went into 'doctor mode' and started checking his pulse and he could hear him breathing. He wanted to resuscitate him but he didn't know how to in this situation and he knew, in the back of his thoughts, Hermes requested 'no resuscitation'.

Hermes was still alive when the cops arrived and didn't die until 1 AM when they decided to call me. I could have been at the hospital with my father in his last moments, but because Satan didn't want me there, they waited until after he died. Sure, I didn't answer the phone at 1, but I might have at 12, I most definitely would have responded to a text that said 'there's an emergency.'

I blatantly asked Balthasar, "Do you think Satan could have done this?" and his response was, "It looks weird and I thought maybe, but I don't want to think like that." So, to me, he clearly had his own suspicions that he pushed away.

I asked about funeral plans again and 'nothing was known at that time' and we hung up the conversation for now.

I now heard two varying stories about how my father died. I knew Satan knew the truth but I didn't want to talk to her and even if I did, she, obviously, was telling different stories and I would not be the one she confided in. Something told me Hermes did not kill himself.

I am not against suicide; I don't like it, and I would rather people have the resources to handle their situations without it, and I want to live a world that doesn't have such devastating situations to bring people to these finalizing actions. However, I don't know people's experiences as well as that person would know their own experience. I know from my happy, optimistic, view on life that I still managed to think suicide was a solution; so it's not beyond my imagination to understand someone with depression, etc. could find those thoughts. Our country (United States) just started a national call line for mental health emergencies, 9-8-8. It's new and I hope it's as helpful as they promise but if for whatever reason its busy or closed, please search out a current number to just talk to someone for a one moment that is willing to listen. Other crisis centers are NAMI, National Suicide Prevention LifeLine, and The Trevor Project- depending on where you live there may be local numbers to call or text.

Hermes may have killed himself, but to me, it was because Satan finally broke him down. 'Breaking him down, to build him up'. Of course, who was she too judge who needed breaking down or to be built up as she sees fit? But besides that, she didn't know how to build things, she was not a creator. She only knew how to break things and destroy people; and she enjoyed it. It, somehow, made her feel better about herself. She didn't want to lift others or herself up, she wanted to wallow in her past aggressions and pull people down to her darkness.

I had escaped. Just like I posted on Facebook, 'I had survived' her, but as I feared, she focused her evil on Hermes, and within two years he was dead. The life sucked out of him by his 'loving' wife who controlled almost every aspect of his days until the only strength he had left was in his trigger finger…IF he, in fact, killed himself.

The day after Hermes death, Sunday, I called in the morning and all three brothers were 'too busy' to talk, but would call me back when they could. They didn't and were 'busy' all day.

Monday, I got a hold of Gaspar and wanted to know if funeral plans had been made yet. Once again he said no. I asked, with annoyance, what was taking soo long and what was happening with Hermes' body. He began to cry and let me know how heavy everything was and he was just lost. I thought Satan's sisters were there to help. He assured me they were helping Satan, but they were NOT helping with the death; apparently Satan was suicidal, another reason she was on sleeping pills.

He explained to me, Hermes' body was 'probably' at the organ donation place by now because Hermes was a donor. I Googled 'What to do when a parent dies?' and made a list of things Gaspar should be doing by now. He thanked me and hung up.

I was worried I was not going to be allowed at the funeral and thought I might be able to see Hermes' body at the organ donation place. When I called them to make an appointment, his body was not there.

The organ donation place said they called all weekend and left messages but no one answered to give them permission to continue the procedure. They said he was still at the morgue. I called the morgue, and they would not let me see his body for made up reasons (the reasons they gave expired and they still wouldn't let me see it.)

I looked up the few insurance places in Long Prairie and found Hermes' lawyer; he did not have a will (at least at the places I uncovered) and had insurance; but there were no directions for a funeral.

I called Gaspar back and let him know where Hermes' body actually was and there was no set funeral will plans. He would have to be on top of it and that's when he told me Satan was a suspect for possible murder and her phone had been taken away so she couldn't answer the organ donation place when they called.

What an interesting detail they had left out over the weekend.

Chapter 20 – A Dire Diagnosis

I try not to share too much opinion or emotion
when talking about this so if I sound short and to the
point, that's because I've disconnected myself from
most of the trauma and because emotions have been
used against me. Since my father's death I have yet to
cry. I've dropped a tear or two but not any big cries,
however, I can feel a lump constantly in my throat. It
wants to come out, I don't mind a good cry, but a part
of me pushes it back done. I am sad, but mainly I'm
angry, I'm angry at the idea of him committing suicide
after telling me what a bad idea that was. I was mad at
the idea of Satan killing him and getting away with it. I
was angry that Satan and her sisters were guarding my
father's last moments from me as if they thought they
were being honorable. I've known this man longer than
any of them and for them to threaten me, that my
'presence wouldn't be welcome' is monstrous of them.
Who keeps a son away from their father's funeral?
Satan does.

I'm also still confused about his death and
working by myself (with Cu Chulainn) to figure out

what I can from anyone willing to talk, but not many people will.

There was sadness too. I was sad my brothers were part of this evil mess. I was sad to have lost the chance to regrow a relationship with my father. I wanted to give him the time, the time I now give to my brothers, to educate himself on queer matters, or abuse, or racism, etc. He was close; he was smart and kind, I believe he could have figured it out.

I also felt vindicated for being called a liar my whole life. Even if Hermes DID kill himself, surely people would see Satan now as the devil she is. But no, my brothers, clung to her side. I was still hopeful, at the time, that I could salvage something with them.

Monday; they, my brothers and Satan's sisters, weaned Satan off the heavy sleeping pills and when I talked to Gaspar on Tuesday, he said she was feeling better. She was still randomly wailing in pain (only during the day time and always out the window facing the town – very controlled outbursts).

Gaspar told me Satan had 'found' a psychiatric note from Hermes' psychologist. She showed it to my brothers hoping it would 'bring more explanation' to Hermes' thought processes. I won't share the specifics from the note but I have four things to say about it:

1. It gave multiple, heavy mental issues to Hermes, and reasoned his suicide: PTSD, Anxiety, Depression, Bipolar, and Attention Deficit Disorder.

2. The note was represented (by Satan) as the 'latest review' on his mental health.

3. Balthasar (the medical student brother) noticed it was not the 'latest review', there had been others since. What it was, was a summary of all his past reviews over his history in the Air Force; not a review of his state before death.

4. The note was taken away within twelve hours by Satan with her saying, "I don't want you guys to think of him in a negative way. Look at these instead," and she

replaced it with love letters from him to her. The psychiatrist's note was never seen again.

To me, it seems like Satan was creating a profile for Hermes to convince people that a.) He was suicidal and b.) He loved her soo much.

I asked, multiple times, for pictures of that diagnoses but it was never sent. Worse yet, I was told in the mix of love letters, there was a letter to me. I assume it would have been when Hermes was at war the second time. I was told I could have the letter, and Balthasar said (like the psychiatric note) that he would get it to me. Spoilers – he does not.

I didn't have to be in Satan's presence to feel the manipulation being pulled over the others. I couldn't trust any of them, not because they were untrustworthy but because they blindly followed Satan; Hermes' downfall. I went around them and called the funeral home in Long Prairie and the funeral had been planned!

The funeral was scheduled for Friday morning; nearly a week after his death. I gave the funeral manager a brief run down about the situation and scheduled a private showing an hour and half before the public funeral. He told me, that worked fine, but he would have to tell Satan. I suggested he shouldn't, for my own sake, but he insisted that it was tradition for the wife to see the husband's body first. I didn't care about tradition nor did I care who saw the body first, but it was not my call.

I knew when he had told Satan, because I was at the dog park and got a phone call from Melchior, but it was Satan instead.

"Tyriel?"

I was in shock and did not answer.

"Tyriel. Hello are you there? He's not there."

"Umm…yes?"

"Oh Tyriel. How are doing?"

"Fine." There was a long silence as she waited for me to ask how she was doing.

"Okay. Well I just wanted to let you know the funerals on Friday at 9 AM. I think your father would like you to come.

"I'm planning on coming."

"Oh...good...I want you to be a pallbear-" She made some muffled noises, and handed the phone to Melchior.

Melchior apologized for her calling on his phone, but then he finished her sentence, letting me know she wants me to be a pallbearer (now that she knew I had my own meeting). The Star Wars meme, "It's a Trap!" was buzzing around my head.

I let Melchior know, I would think about it but I wanted to be very clear that I did not want to engage with Satan or any of here minions. I said, "I understand we will be in the same room, but I do NOT want to interact with her. If she can be okay with that, I will continue to consider it." He agreed and after I got off the phone I thought about it more with Cu Chulainn.

I wanted to be a pallbearer. There was something symbolic about carrying your father to his final resting place, and I would be doing it with my brothers.

I made a plan to stay a day or two after to see if I could have a dinner with my brothers, while we were all together, so I called back, Gaspar this time, and agreed to be a pallbearer and got the color of suit needed to match with them. I let him know, I was going to come up Thursday, and was hoping we could get together, but like every other time I mentioned 'coming up', it was ignored. Regardless of their lack of response, Cu Chulainn and I drove the two hours, the day before the funeral, to Long Prairie.

I was going back to my personal hell, to participate in a nightmare with Satan.

Chapter 21 – Xtra Xeroxes

While on our way to Long Prairie, I sent a text message to my brother's letting them know I was on my way. I would stay at a fast-food place in town and sit there until it closes and if any of them wanted to come and see me, I would be there; 'no obligations.' I added, I was going to keep my hotel room till Sunday if they wanted to get together after the hecticness of the funeral. They could make sure Satan is fine, and we could go out to eat; just the four brothers. Still no response from them, but I did get a phone call from my aunt, Coatlicue. She was asking if I would be at the funeral and I let her know I would be and was planning on pallbearing.

At first, I was not sure what to expect from her; we hadn't talked since my Facebook post. The lack of communication was my doing. I left everyone from both sides of the family for two reasons;

1.) I assumed, wrongly, they shared the same views as my family. My family hated gay people, I was a gay, so I was avoiding my family AND others I thought had the same mindset. Satan had told me if I had grown up with my aunt she would have "beat the gay out of me senselessly" so I was lucky to be with her (Satan claiming herself to be someone who was using "God's power" to remove the sin). 'Senselessly' is the keyword she was using there. Anywho, my apprehensions where dismissed immediately as she started going in on Satan.

And the other reason I avoided them -

2.) I didn't want there to be third parties telling my father how I was doing. I wanted Hermes to pick up the phone and call me himself and I knew if I was still talking with my aunt or even a second cousin twice removed, it would get back to him. Hermes was a primary caretaker in a small town, if I talked to a gas attendant he would hear about it. So I stopped conversations with all family but I let Hermes and my brothers know the door was open; and only them.

Now with Hermes dead, I didn't know who or why I was keeping people out.

Side note: Hermes had a coronary bypass half a year to me disconnecting. It was one of the reasons we had started having monthly meetings. Fortunately he was very close to retirement at 60 and finished out whatever work contract he had. He was in the process of doing this when I removed myself.

Coatlicue divulged to me, that Hermes, after retirement, did not want to depend on his funds for all the bills and Satan would have to continue working to soften the pay until it was time for her to retire. Coatlicue witnessed Satan threaten and plead, to not work, constantly to Hermes when they got drunk together (which was constantly.)

No offense to drinkers, as long as you're responsible and respectful, do what you will. That being said, Coatlicue was a heavy drinker. I don't know if she would consider herself an alcoholic or not but she matched many of the criteria, Satan was also a heavy drinker and stashed little bottles in her purse and under the bed, and as a past alcoholic, I see the signs.

Hermes, also, rarely was seen without a beer in his hand after noon. Satan and Hermes did not consider their drinking a problem but Satan coped with it by drinking with Coatlicue to make fun of her and make herself feel like she didn't have a problem, in comparison to Coatlicue.

Coatlicue had become one of Satan's punching bags in the disguise of having a 'tough family love'.

Coatlicue explained during these drunken hang outs how Satan was not letting Hermes do anything anymore, "If I can't have free time, he doesn't get any." When she was sober, or less drunk, or in front of Hermes, she would correct the narrative and say, "...because of his bypass. He can't be doing anything."

It was understandable for her to deny him the next season of cows or make him sell the horses. Those are big animals, they take a lot of work, and demand constant hours of care. But to deny him chickens, ducks, pheasants, or even just a pig. Hermes had a dog already and he refused to let him go, but Satan also attacked his hobbies. He wasn't allowed to go bowling, and he couldn't play 'corn hole'. A game similar to horseshoes with small bags of corn or sand, and holes instead of poles; a yard game.

Coatlicue said Hermes mentioned divorce but was afraid to be deemed a failure and find himself alone again. Hermes was thinking about divorce and vocalizing it out loud in a small town. She said Hermes was at her house, during the daytimes, helping out around the house and yard and was planning to build a short fence to separate her garden from the neighbor's yard.

When he was over there he would complain about how hard it was living with Satan. Later, in the nights, Satan would come over and complain how annoying it was living with Hermes, with him there all the time now. The complaints were always laughed off.

Coatlicue also mentioned Hermes' health was fine, it wasn't 100% back, but they talked about it throughout the healing process and Hermes said he was at 90%. My father was stoic so it might have been closer to 80% but if he was going out of his way to help Coatlicue at her home, rather than staying home, it doesn't seem as likely. Unless he didn't care how much pain he was in and still wanted to get away from Satan. I could see that.

Coatlicue remembered Satan the night of Hermes' death. She was already drunk when she came over and was pissed about going to their grandson's birthday party; she was bad mouthing Hermes. She continued to get further wasted. Balthasar, in his retelling also said she came home wasted.

We finished up our conversation happy to be talking again. She said, "I was a better mother to you than she ever was." While this may be true, the word 'mother' made me cringe.

Cu Chulainn and I got a hotel room from a town neighboring Long Prairie, keeping our distance. While unpacking we realized the funeral suits had been left at home and Cu Chulainn would have to go back to get there after dropping me off at the fast food place. I was counting on Cu Chulainn to be my safety escape if Satan's sisters decided to attack or if my anxiety got the best of me, but I would be stuck at the restaurant for at least four hours if not longer.

I took the time to write, as I do, a long, long letter to Hermes. It was in a small yellow journal made of recycled paper I got from a renaissance fair. I nearly filled the whole book up when Balthasar walked in.

Chapter 22 – An Encouraging Encounter

We hugged and it was nice for a moment to see my brother. He seemed restrained and I soon realized this was not a meeting of brothers happy to reminisce on their father and cry together over their loss. I was about to be put on trial to see if I was "worth" bringing back into the family.

Balthasar knew I was atheist (I'd say agnostic) but he didn't really know the difference or how anyone could be either anyway, like I said, we grew up catholic. However, he felt obligated to tell me before anything else, "I claim Jesus as my Lord and Savior, and I am becoming Christian. I believe he [Jesus] died for my sins and through him I can be a better person." He went on to explain how he got a sign from Hermes' hot tub, and since he and Hermes had been sitting in the hot tub the night Hermes died... it must be Jesus. I told him that logic worried me, but if that was a path he was wanted, he should look into 'apologetics', a common tool to defend Christian beliefs, AND then he should look up rebuttals to those apologetics.

I'd say he's capable of figuring out the inconsistencies of religious thinking, but in this same conversation he told me; 'women are not as logical as men', 'gay is a sin but he doesn't hate the sinner', and he doesn't 'get the trans-phenomenon'.

There was soo much stupidity flying around me I couldn't begin to address any of it, and I wasn't there to correct his view points. I was flabbergasted by the nonchalantnous of his ideals being revealed, as if, he was letting me know what he was okay with and not okay with. I just told him, if God is something important to him than I think he should research it like he would, hopefully, do for anything that is important.

The day Hermes died and I told him to get a therapist I know I told him a 'secular' one. I suspect he went and talked to his school counselor, who I also assume is Christian, because the phrase I quoted above from him, is not a sentence he came up with in his head or something hot tub-Jesus bubbled up. It's a common phrase Christians say. He didn't say it word for word, but I've worked with enough Christians and ex Christians to recognize it. I could also tell throughout the conversation he was prepped with responses.

He scripted to me, "This time has been stressful, for everyone, and tensions are high. Jesus is helping me through this time and I wanted to come to you with peace and let you know, right away, that I love you."

I responded, "Christianity is not overly welcoming to the queer community but I love you also." I changed the subject, annoyed at the feeling of being preached to. "Do we know anything new about father?"

It was a very open ended question and I was expecting more funeral information, but instead he gave the THIRD version of Satan's ever changing tale. This is the most sober telling from Satan but keep in mind it's her story filtered through Balthasar and now filtered through me:

After Satan got home from Coatlicue's, the night of the death of Hermes, Balthasar had gone to bed; Satan and Hermes started arguing right away, IN the house. Hermes walked away from her grabbing his slippers to go outside, where she FOLLOWED him all the down to the barn.

She says they continued the argument in the barn, admitting she was in and out of a blacked out state. Hermes pulled a gun, "from out of nowhere" and he shot himself, in the head, before saying, "Well. Then how about this?"

And that was it.

Hermes was found in his slippers, and in the barn. To paint the picture better; my father's barn was also his rec room. He had a paved and closed off section with a reclining chair and big screen-television, a mini fridge and bar.

My brother's claim Hermes would never have walked down on the muddy driveway when he had a 4-wheeler he would have used.

I think, he went outside to avoid her, and was not intending on going down to the barn until she followed him outside. My father would walk in slippers in the mud just to piss her off, because he knew there were his and he could do that. I can see her continuing to berate him and follow him down to the barn as he was trying to avoid the situation, literally trudging in the dark to get to his safe place, and she wouldn't let him have it.

I told Balthasar, the story has changed a few times and it sounds weird. He agreed but didn't want to think about it. He went the other way and began to tell me how he was suspicious of the police and thought they could be 'framing' Satan. The police, for me, have not been a part of this story other than after Hermes' death and they haven't shared anything, good or bad, so I asked him why he would think this.

Apparently, our middle brother, Melchior, who was in law enforcement, didn't trust the small town police because when he was 19, nearly ten years ago, he was at a high school bonfire party that got busted by the cops and he ran from them, drunk, in a cornfield until he was tackled and then he punched one of the cops. The cop he punched now worked for the Long Prairie department.

I attempted to steel man the story, "You think the police are framing mom because Melchior was an idiot kid a decade ago and punched one of the cops?"

He told me that they, Satan and co., are letting Melchior deal with police because of that situation and because he has experienced in the field and Melchior had suggested they NOT deal with the police at all.

The sheriff had been to the house asking questions and requesting items that could help determine whether it was murder or suicide. Things like, permission to access the Alexa, the psychiatric note, additional retellings of the story, passwords to the CAMERA in the barn and the door cams!

I stopped the conversation, "There's footage!?"

Balthasar once again let me down when he told me the camera in the barn had been unplugged the day BEFORE, by Satan. She wanted to watch the dogs play in the house when she was not there. To me it was the lamest excuse to set up a camera in the house when 1.) They have had the dogs for years, why the sudden interest. 2.) There are other closer, easier cameras to set up. 3.) The camera never moved from the barn, it was merely unplugged and left there.

Every piece of information I uncover screams that Satan is not just a murderer, but possible planned it. I gave Balthasar another skeptical look.

And he was done with thinking about the possibilities. He ended the conversation and said, "I didn't come to talk about this. Right now we need to focus on healing and this could be an opportunity for you to come back to the family, Satan misses you, and we all forgive you."

Chapter 23 – Vetting for Vitals

"Pardon?" I asked, "What am I being forgiven for?"

"For hurting Satan in the past by spreading rumors, even if you believed them."

I asked for clarity and he referenced my Facebook post. "Do you know what my post was about?"

He said he had read it but didn't remember what it said, "You were angry at mom for not accepting your lifestyle choices."

I realized Satan had just turned my post into a lie. It didn't matter what it said, the abuse, the feelings, the goodbye, it had all been summed up as 'a lie' and that is all my brothers remembered. That was how strong her influence was over them; she could rewrite history. As another more popular evil villain in our midst once said; she could have shot Hermes point blank in the middle of town and they would let her get away with it. They were willing to help her.

"I'm sorry, Balthasar, you don't know the situation, and I'm not apologizing for anything."

He then informed me, this could be my "last chance to have a family."

"Balthasar. I have a family and I don't think Hermes would be happy with an ultimatum during his funeral. I would like to build a relationship with you, Melchior and Gaspar (two people who didn't ever show up.)" Melchior was not 'feeling up to it' and Gaspar's kid wasn't 'feeling well', despite his wife, Satan, and Satan's sisters being there to help babysit. "I will never engage with that woman again. She is abusive, and she is abusive to me, in particular."

He stood up angry, threatening to punch me with a clenched fist and blamed me for not listening and not trying to. I let him know if he was going to apologize for me, he can save it. There was a short outburst giving me my final ultimatum; I denied it and he left.

I DID give an apology to the cashier that was cleaning up, and called Cu Chulainn to calm down. He was on his way back and picked me up.

I was glad I didn't cancel my private meeting with Hermes' body the next morning. I was no longer going to be a pallbearer or attend the public service. I traveled two hours to get 5 minutes from my brothers and two of the three couldn't bother to say hi, and the only one that did, came on mission to drag me back to hell.

I got up early the day of the funeral and got dressed in my suit, even though I didn't need it. I headed to the funeral before the people prepping for the public showing arrived.

The funeral manager let me in and showed me to the coffin. There he was; his husk.

It looked nothing like him. Like a wax doll or a ventriloquist dummy. My eyes couldn't help but look for an entry or exit-hole cover up. I pulled out my book I wrote the day before and started reading it, trying to be in the moment. I couldn't focus on the words. I looked for a place I could leave the book without it being discovered. I asked the manager for suggestions and he placed the book in Hermes' inside jacket pocket. He told me the body was to be burned and assured me the book would be burned with it. I took a last moment, said my goodbye, and left.

Since then;

Satan has given away Hermes' things to my brothers and her sisters. She has held garage sales, and was trying to sell the house. While she's under investigation for his murder, she is not entitled to his Air Force retirement, insurance, and/or if there is one, his will. She had managed to suck every last drop of life out of him. She was only having trouble selling the house because Hermes had made a deal with a neighbor that placed part of the house on the neighbor's land, and Satan would have to make a deal with the neighbor now to close that deal first. The neighbor didn't like Satan so it's been a stand still as of the publishing of this book.

Satan changed the story for a fourth time with her 'now remembering'; *Hermes pulled the gun out from behind a cabinet and she actually wrestled with him, both of their hands getting on the gun, before he shot himself.* To me, Melchior, as the law enforcement 'advice' took into consideration the GSR (Gun Shot Residue) report may come back positive on Satan's hands, and having her wrestling the gun would help explain why.

She has changed the story two more times. I reconnected with my grandma (Hermes' mother) and aunt Coatlicue and they have been keeping me in the loop with the investigation. The three of us have been calling the sheriff's department and sharing what we hear, but I stopped listening to the versions from Satan. I, hate to, believe that there won't be enough evidence to show the truth of that night, and since I believe she killed him, I'm afraid she will get away with it; another reason for me to write this memoir and share my OPINION on this matter.

Before my Facebook post I wanted to talk with Satan. After my post, I still kept the door open for her as well as my father, just not as wide; I imagined giving her a 60 second timer to apologize and explain what she was apologizing for. But after Hermes death I have no reason to connect with her. Hermes was the only thing driving and connecting me to Satan. I don't care when she dies, how she dies, where she dies, etc. I just hope, until then, every time she closes her eyes she sees the image of a dead Hermes engraved on the back of her eye lids, I hope she can feel the scrapping of the scarred image sliding past her iris when she wakes, I hope it hurts and I hope when she looks in the mirror she sees the monster I saw when I was 9 years old as she abused me; the face she tries to hide from everyone else, AND I hope she knows everyone can see it now.

I, since, have requestioned my relationship with Hermes and 'pride', the pride most children aspire to get from their parents. I discovered a distrust I have for people that I didn't think I had before, or maybe it grew as I realized I had been accurate on her character. I was relieved to be done with her, and thankful to revisit relationships with my father's side. Grateful for my husband and dog (and my cat) - not enough mention or credit for the cat!

I'm also thankful to get this out of my head. I can put this book on my shelf and know it's there without having to open it. I'll never have to speak on it again, I can just point to a book, and if someone cares enough they can read it. I will no longer have to relive this trauma.

Chapter 24 – Critical Crime Thinking

Here are my final thoughts on the limited scenarios orbiting the death of Hermes:

<u>If Hermes was planning on killing himself</u> that night, here are some of the signs I found that could have signaled it;

Hermes may have waited for the week when Balthasar was visiting so that he could see him one more time. He took a 'farewell' tour to Gaspar and Melchior's family-but then why wait till three days later and the evening before an additional visit (the birthday party)? Also why not wait till Balthasar goes back to college? One wouldn't want a medical student around to reverse the action.

I can, take my emotions, out of it, and try to understand why he wouldn't have added me to his visiting list, but not write a letter ahead of time or a text. I doubt he didn't consider me, but maybe he still chose not to reach out.

Maybe his psychiatric note was legit, his mind and/or his body was in pain after the bypass. If he had been living with those for years, why shoot yourself three days before Satan's birthday (the 5th of April) and on the day of his grandson's birthday?

Why plan out a suicide, only to do it in the heat of the moment with a person in front of you, who could possible help or call for help?

Lastly, the argument, that was held all week (between Hermes and Satan), was about going to this party. Why would he plan to kill himself if his side of the argument was that he WANTED to go? Why would he be arguing about it in the first place, if he knew he wasn't planning on making it? If he was annoyed with Satan, he wouldn't have spent his last week creating a fake argument, just to die the night before.

I do NOT believe it was a planned suicide, but maybe it was not planned, but still could have been suicide;

Hermes was drunk, maybe not wasted but he had been drinking. Balthasar said he drank less than normal nights, but a hot tub can increase inebriation. He had been out of the tub for about an hour before his death, although that doesn't mean he didn't keep drinking.

Could Hermes have just had enough of Satan and felt trapped in life and literally trapped in the barn with a human sized life-leech? It would have clearly been out of spite and/or annoyance of Satan, since his last words, according to her, were, "Well. Then how about this?"

What a person will do in the spur moment of an anxious 'fight or flight' situation is, unfortunately, the variable that keeps the door cracked open to suicide. No one knows for sure what Hermes was thinking. If he thought that was his way out, he must have felt it was his ONLY option. Maybe there will be a law that criminalizes the type of abuses that lead to these devastating thoughts and permanent actions in the future, but here we are now.

<u>IF Satan planned to murder Hermes;</u>

Satan knew Hermes had a retirement plan for her. If anything happened to him he had paid off most the bills and she could sell the land and take his insurance (he said it should be a comfy one million dollars) and Satan could move to Texas with her sisters where she could continue getting his Air Force after pay. Hermes, as the proud provider, had told me and multiple others this. We also knew Satan wanted soo badly to retire, it was a common topic with increased volume. She also openly hated Minnesota, but that was not new. That's motive enough.

Another motive was of course the birthday party she was reluctant to go to and her control she felt she had to maintain over her presentation.

Also, Hermes mentioned divorce to Coatlicue and if that got back to Satan via small town rumors, her ego would have been devastated.

She has a history of abuse (mental, physical, and sexual), and history of lying, along with changing the story of his death over five times. Also, she and her son's admit to keeping evidence from the police to "protect her." And she knew where the gun was kept, regardless of knowing where it 'popped' out of, so the means are there also.

She unplugged the only camera in the room within 24 hours of his death and didn't call the police herself; she waited until Balthasar came down to the barn for him to call. And we know she was heavily intoxicated, admitting herself she was in and out of "blacking out."

Could Hermes have committed suicide?

Yes.

Is it likely?

No, I can explain away 99% of the evidence pointing to suicide.

<u>Did Satan simply come home wasted, and shoot Hermes out of rage?</u>

Seems drastically more likely. But, I agree with the court system, that it needs to be 100% likely, so I have to hope, eventually, if this case is ever closed, there is a piece of evidence out there somewhere that shows the truth, whatever that truth may be.

Chapter 25 – Agitated Advice

My final words to the people involved.

To my father's side of the family;

Our theme for new people when they enter our family is, "if they can shell back the crap we throw at them, they will fit in just fine." This creates a safe zone for assholes instead of their victims. Satan should have never felt comfortable enough to make fun of people's weight, color, class, relationship, IQ, etc. The fact the she got away with this in front of 'friends' and 'family' is disgusting. We should understand defending someone's identity (things they cannot change about themselves) by calling out a loved one, is not being nosey or butting into someone's relationship. It's shutting down bullying.

We need to understand, being called a racist or sexist, is about your actions, not your person, and if you truly want to be a better person, get over the offensiveness of those words and find out why one might perceive you that way.

I know a lot of you don't want to talk to me. You don't know me other than what Satan has told you and I left rather than defending myself to you, so maybe I'm not worth the time to get to know now. I misjudged most of you based on my upbringing, and am aware of that, I still don't know you very well either, but I'm willing to meet each of you with a clean slate if you want and are willing to do the same with me.

To Satan's sisters;

Following the bible without ever having read it, is stupid.

To Satan;

I've wasted enough ink.

To my brothers;

None of you deserve his last name for the betrayal you added in his final moments, and carrying it is the actual April's Fool's joke.

The door is still open. It might not have a flowery 'welcome' sign, but it is open. I understand why you love the way you do. I was there when you were raised and I know the thinking processes you were taught. I obviously don't know your thoughts now, or how you viewed those lessons, but it took me a long time to find healthy messages in the abuse. We can learn things together.

If you read this, I hope you read the last paragraph to Hermes' side of the family. You are not bigots, yet, but your actions are racist, homophobic, sexist, etc. It's not your fault, but it will be, now that you know, if you continue not do anything about it.

You risk replicating the same dangerous and sad marriage our parents had and there will be more suicides and/or murders. It's already too late for some of you to do the homework BEFORE having children, but since you have chosen to have kids without learning how to raise them first, it's more important than ever that you start doing research on the fundamental things you should have learnt before parroting what are parents told us.

I dealt with loosing Hermes' pride, years before he died. I understand how lost it feels to be striving to meet someone else's goal and then for it to suddenly seem meaningless. I know the confusion and the feeling of not knowing where to go next. I figured out how to handle those thoughts isolated from the family. I hope you have healthy support, and I'm here if you decide you need more help.

To Hermes;

I'm sorry for whatever part my leaving had on your mental health, whether it be depression or the abuse caused by Satan. I wish you could have realized, through our conversations and my life, you could have also left. I wish you could have seen that I'm not only happy without Satan in my life, but doing well. I like to think you would be proud, if it still mattered and I wish we could have been friends. I'm sorry we didn't make it and I hope this book makes of for it.

You were in a dark spot that sniffed out your light but you changed many others with your warmth before it was stolen. I may not have agreed with your moral direction but your compass was true and I like to think I got my drive to be a better person from you. Your light shines strong in me.

I don't know where your body/ashes are; Guarded by Satan. She took everything from you and me, so it would only make sense she would keep your body and not tell me the location. But I have your memory;

I built you a statue, like one of the Pompeii statues from my wedding. It sits like you and will be in my garden, outside among nature, as you liked to be. Eventually, I'll get chickens and your statue can protect over them like the farmer you were. It has 'a wind spinner' in the chest so when a breeze catches it, it feels like you may be near. It's decorated with colorful leaves and mosses and an owl rests where your head ought to be; to remind me of how I lost you and for the wisdom you had, but I questioned.

Thank you father, I love you.

To me;

I hope the investigation ends soon and I can have some mental peace. I hope my brothers take the time to educate themselves and will want to reach out, but I have no expectations and I don't plan on waiting around. I will continue to try and be a better person, both discovering what that means to me, and how to be it for my community and my new family. I need to be proud of myself when I lay my head down. I love life and there is lots to learn. I hope I can keep my yearning for discovery alive while still being aware of the harmful aspects to avoid.

Chapter 26 – Undone Units

If and when the investigation ends, I will release a version that has the result here.